Praise for *Designing and Engineering Time*

"Seow has written the definitive book about understanding and engineering the perception of time in user experience. It is clear, engaging, and thorough. This is a must-read for designers, developers, or anyone else who makes decisions regarding the interaction of humans and computers."

—Susan Hodges Ramlet, Interaction Design Engineer
Member, Usability Professionals' Association

"The first comprehensive guide to this very important aspect of software usability. Chock-full of tangible examples and great techniques. Accessible for all members of the software development team and business sponsors too."

—Terrence Michael Gardiner, theTEAMcompany.com
Owner and Principal User-Centered Design Consultant

"If you're browsing for a book that explains why users are so frustrated with your software, this is it. If you're looking for ways to eliminate those frustrations, then buy this book."

—Tim Patrick, author of *Programming Visual Basic 2008*

"Response time is one of the most important contributors to user satisfaction with a system. The slow system seems recalcitrant to the point of defiance. It provokes multiple clicking, and if too slow, the user abandons it. Beyond just making performance better, engineers, system architects, and usability practitioners need to understand how users perceive time and how a well-designed system will exploit that understanding. In *Designing and Engineering Time*, Steve presents a scholarly yet very readable book on the perception of time and its design implications. This book is destined to become a classic."

—Dennis Wixon, Ph.D., User Research Manager, Microsoft Games Studios

Designing and Engineering Time

Designing and Engineering Time

The Psychology of Time Perception in Software

Steven C. Seow, Ph.D.

✦✦ Addison-Wesley

Upper Saddle River, NJ • Boston • Indianapolis • San Francisco

New York • Toronto • Montreal • London • Munich • Paris • Madrid

Cape Town • Sydney • Tokyo • Singapore • Mexico City

Many of the designations used by manufacturers and sellers to distinguish their products are claimed as trademarks. Where those designations appear in this book, and the publisher was aware of a trademark claim, the designations have been printed with initial capital letters or in all capitals.

The author and publisher have taken care in the preparation of this book, but make no expressed or implied warranty of any kind and assume no responsibility for errors or omissions. No liability is assumed for incidental or consequential damages in connection with or arising out of the use of the information or programs contained herein.

The publisher offers excellent discounts on this book when ordered in quantity for bulk purchases or special sales, which may include electronic versions and/or custom covers and content particular to your business, training goals, marketing focus, and branding interests. For more information, please contact:

U.S. Corporate and Government Sales
(800) 382-3419
corpsales@pearsontechgroup.com

For sales outside the United States, please contact:

International Sales
international@pearsoned.com

This Book Is Safari Enabled

The Safari® Enabled icon on the cover of your favorite technology book means the book is available through Safari Bookshelf. When you buy this book, you get free access to the online edition for 45 days.

Safari Bookshelf is an electronic reference library that lets you easily search thousands of technical books, find code samples, download chapters, and access technical information whenever and wherever you need it.

To gain 45-day Safari Enabled access to this book:

· Go to http://www.awprofessional.com/safarienabled.
· Complete the brief registration form.
· Enter the coupon code LMQK-I81P-9I91-3XQI-C78Y.

If you have difficulty registering on Safari Bookshelf or accessing the online edition, please e-mail customer-service@safaribooksonline.com.

Visit us on the Web: www.awprofessional.com

Library of Congress Cataloging-in-Publication Data:
Seow, Steve.
  Designing and engineering time : the psychology of time perception in software / Steve Seow. — 1st ed.
    p. cm.
  ISBN 0-321-50918-8 (pbk. : alk. paper) 1. Software engineering. 2. Human-computer interaction— Psychological aspects. 3. User-centered system design 4. Time perception. I. Title.
  QA76.758.S456 2008
  005.1—dc22

                                                              2008003570

ISBN-13: 978-0-321-50918-5
ISBN-10: 0-321-50918-8
Text printed in the United States on recycled paper at RR Donnelley in Crawfordsville, Indiana.
First printing May 2008

Editor-in-Chief
Karen Gettman

Acquisitions Editor
Chris Guzikowski

Development Editor
Chris Zahn

Managing Editor
Gina Kanouse

Project Editor
Meg Shaw

Copy Editor
Keith Cline

Indexer
Cheryl Lenser

Proofreader
Jovana San Nicolas-Shirley

Publishing Coordinator
Raina Chrobak

Book Designer
Anne Jones

Compositor
Nonie Ratcliff

For Jaime, my wife, and Alex, my son.

Contents

Acknowledgments

I would like to first thank the very competent editorial staff at Addison-Wesley, specifically Karen Gettman, Joan Murray, Chris Guzikowski, Emily Frey, Meg Shaw, and Raina Chrobak, who hand-held me through the process of writing my first book. Second, a big thank you (on behalf of the readers, too) must go to the reviewers—Bernard Farrell, Mark Friedman, Terry Gardiner, Tim Patrick, and Susan Ramlet—whose comments helped prevent this book from turning into a textbook. I would also like to thank my talented colleagues at Microsoft, particularly Mark Friedman, who not only provided valuable feedback, but also put many of the concepts in this book to test and to practice.

About the Author

Steven C. Seow joined Microsoft as a User Researcher after completing his Ph.D. in Experimental Psychology at Brown University with a research focus on human timing. Prior to Brown, the Singapore native completed his Bachelor's and Master's degrees in Forensic Psychology at John Jay College of Criminal Justice with a thesis examining the distortion of time perception. Steven constantly confers with colleagues across his company to talk about time and timing issues. Coupled with his scholarly interest in psychology is his passion for computer technology. In his spare time, Steven enjoys tinkering with computer hardware, dabbling with programming languages, and building websites. He lives in Maple Valley, Washington, with his wife and son.

For more information about Steven, visit his website at www.StevenSeow.com.

Preface

This book was written with several practitioners and professionals in mind. The first group is the software engineers. Not everyone has had the opportunity (or wants) to take classes in human-computer interaction, usability, or user interface design, and not every company can afford to hire usability professionals to assist with optimizing the user friendliness of a website or the discoverability of the new features of an application. If you are a developer or an architect, you are one for a good reason: Your magic and craft is turning ones and zeros into a solution that makes life and work better. However, just as it is good to know what to do if you get a flat tire and not rely on a mechanic, it is good for you to be able to apply simple concepts to improve the usability and appeal of your solution.

The second group of readers I had in mind consists of usability professionals. This group includes a subset of my colleagues at Microsoft whose job responsibilities and talent make them the "voice of the user" to the rest of the company to ensure that our products and services are easy to use, easy to learn, and so on. If you are like my colleagues, you care not only about how a product or service is used or consumed, but also how it is perceived, what emotions it may conjure up, and what behaviors it may cause. This book provides the research, the logic, and other useful knowledge to help you understand how to deal with and correct usability issues arising from time and timing.

A third group of readers is everyone else who has some responsibility to ensure that a solution is delivered with quality and value. This includes program and product managers, testers, marketing professionals, and all other decision makers involved in putting a solution in front of the user. Reality is such that we have to make tradeoffs, compromises, and workarounds. Reality also dictates that we work with the resources that we have. This book takes that into consideration and provides as much practical guidance as possible on how to set reasonable and informed tradeoffs.

Regardless of your background, one of the characteristics of this book that will catch your attention is the mishmash of information, anecdotes, examples, theories, and practices from a variety of disciplines and industries well beyond the purview of software engineering and human-computer interaction: service and retail, food and beverage, culinary, psychology, sociology, animal research, business management, entertainment, banking, and communication, just to name a few. This eclectic presentation reflects the essence of the topic of the book—the multiple facets and universal experience of time.

This human experience of time is difficult to describe, let alone improve for the human-computer interaction. This is where leveraging knowledge from other disciplines and industries becomes vital. For example, one of my earliest epiphanies about managing the experience of time came when I was standing in the checkout line at a local Costco. While standing in line, I noticed a store employee brandishing a scanner gun and furiously zapping the merchandise in the shopping cart of a customer in front of me. When she was done, she accosted me and demanded to see my Costo card. I surrendered my card, which she zapped with the gun in a split second, before she started rummaging through my merchandise. She hunted and zapped the UPC codes within a few seconds, and when she scanned the last item, proceeded to ditch me like she did with the guy in front of me. Not known for being shy, I asked her point-blank, "What did you just do?" She nonchalantly explained that she had just rung my items up and that all I have to do when I get to the cashier is pay. Skeptical of how that works and worried that I might end up paying for someone else's merchandise, I quizzed her about how the cashier would know which group of merchandise is mine. She looked at me over her drooping reading glasses, waved the gun, and replied that she had scanned my card.

A few seconds after she walked away without giving any time for a follow-up question, it dawned on me how brilliant an idea that was. Sure enough, when I got to the register, the cashier simply scanned my card and announced how much I needed to pay. My merchandise went from the shelf, suffered a little manhandling, and straight into the trunk of my car. Costco has effectively made very intelligent use of my waiting time and has expedited my check-out process!

It wasn't long after my Costco experience that I realized that these proven techniques are applicable to the design of computer software. Why can't we ask the users all the questions up front and then proceed to start the lengthy installation? Why can't we load what users want to use immediately and then continue to load other features that are less important in the background? Why can't we provide instructions on how to use a product while the product is installing? We can, and we sometimes do, but not nearly enough because we keep seeing users throw their hands up in the air in frustration and hear them describe an application, website, or some computer as "stupid." How can this be?

At the time of this writing, the microprocessor found in the average home personal computer can perform billions of instructions per second. That is a lot of *brain* power. Surely, the computer cannot be stupid. What users are telling us is not that the computer doesn't have enough *brains,* but that it doesn't have enough *mind.* We are talking about having enough mind to be cognizant of what is important and valuable to the user, enough mind to be clear and proper about communicating to the user, and enough mind to be considerate and intelligent about how a user's time is expensed efficiently.

This book, like a spin-off or sequel to the *Wizard of Oz,* is attempting to give the computer a mind (or more accurately, more of it). The objective of this book is to ensure that the user experience is *expeditious.* This is done by not blindly applying what has worked for other people, but to go one step further to understand why it works. I have divided the chapters into two essential parts. The first is organized by topic and provides specific knowledge, guidance, and other recommendations on issues pertaining to perception, user tolerance, responsiveness, detecting differences, progress indication, expressing time, and so forth. The second part comprises two compilations. The first is a compilation of proven techniques culled from psychological principles, business practices, industry research, and other sources. (Yes, you will find a technique here that speaks to my Costco experience.) The second is a compilation of violations that comprises the user experience in terms of how time and perception was managed. Here you will find some painfully familiar practices, such as the Time-Fluctuation Phenomenon mentioned by *PC Magazine*'s John C. Dvorak.

I hope that this book will elicit from you two responses that I get when I give talks related to the subject matter. The first is *schadenfreude*—a form of pleasure that you get from the misfortune of other people. This is commonly expressed by my audience as laughter when I relate the pain that people have to experience as a result of bad design in products and services. The second is the *bobble-head effect*—the approving nods from the audience, typically seen well before I deliver the punch line or finish describing an anecdote. Both are positive signs for me as a speaker because they indicate that the audience identifies with what they are hearing. So, if you find yourself somewhat giggly or catch yourself nodding your head as you read this book, then, to me, this book has earned its keep.

Designing and Engineering Time

Every interaction with the computer—from performing a search for information in a database that may last a few seconds to installing an operating system that can last for hours—requires users to *expend* time. How an interaction is designed to expend a user's time is a vital factor in the usability and overall perception of a product or service. A poorly-designed solution can, simply put, waste the user's time regardless of its brilliant architecture. A well-designed user solution, on the other hand, can win user satisfaction despite annoying delays.

Sounds Familiar?

It's five minutes until lunch time and you start an installation process that is supposed to take more than an hour. Not wanting to sit in front of the LCD screen to watch the entire installation process, you cheerfully click a button clearly labeled Install Now! You click the button and leave for lunch. You return from lunch an hour later, satiated and optimistic. However, instead of seeing a congratulatory message proclaiming that installation was successful, you see a dialog box asking whether you really, really want to proceed with the installation.

You are downloading a fairly large file over the Internet. The progress indication on the user interface (UI) suggests that there is only five seconds remaining. You decide to stick around and witness the final moments of the download. Sure enough, the remaining seconds tick: four, three, two, one, zero. You are ecstatic because you have waited a long time for this download—an update patch for a game that promises to give you a new set of weapons, specifically the new photon…wait, the UI is reporting zero…zero…zero….

These excruciating encounters aren't that uncommon. There is no short supply of examples of poor design around us that invoke the same emotions as the one that makes us want to punch something or pull our hair out. Search for "man angry at computer" on the Internet for a short video clip that captures an extreme display of what poor user experience can do to users. Fortunately, there are many ways in which you can minimize the chances of your user reaching the state of frustration shown in the video. This book doesn't contain instructions to build a time machine to accelerate delays in your solution, but it comes pretty close: It consolidates all the knowledge, research, and practice to help you *design* and *engineer* time to turn an otherwise annoying delay into a pleasant pause, or make something that is unbearably long feel like a fleeting duration.

The Funny Thing about Time

Sermonizing about *time* attracts a crowd as diverse as that of experts who flock to study the Shroud of Turin: almost every imaginable scientific discipline and nonscientific group has an invested interest in understanding time. Philosophy, as a prime example, has been concerned with time for more than 2,500 years. Consider the following quandary: When is the *present* or what we call *now*? Three seconds after we proclaim *now, now* has essentially expired into *then*.[1] When is now, then?

---

[1] This paradox is termed *specious present*. Originally coined by E. R. Clay and broached by a man regarded by many as the father of American psychology, William James, in his seminal work, *Principles of Psychology*.

Since its birth in the late 1800s, psychology has focused on using reaction time—the time taken to make a simple response (say a finger tap) to the appearance of a stimulus (say a dot that appears on a screen)—as a measure to investigate behavior. For example, one of the scientists who pioneered the use of time is F. C. Donders, who recorded people's reaction times to simple stimulus (such as pressing a key as soon as a red dot appears) and choice-reaction times (such as pressing a key when a red dot appears, but not when a blue one appears). The time taken by people to make simple decisions[2] is found by just subtracting simple-reaction time from choice-reaction time. Today, time measurement remains a popular choice for behavioral scientists to measure and infer mental processes.

Time can also be an easy and useful factor to manipulate (most typically by delaying), to assess behavior, and to infer cognitive processes. One of the earliest experimental attempts to use time in this way is the classic 1885 memory experiment conducted by H. Ebbinghaus, who is regarded by many as the father of memory research. Ebbinghaus systematically studied and described the forgetting of remembered information in memory over time by manipulating the length of time before people were asked to recall nonsense syllables (such as FQR, GYW, etc.), earning him the reputation of being the first to coin the term *learning curve*.

Many other disciplines have significant contributions to the understanding of time: physics, chemistry, neuroscience, archeology, geology, and so on. Each discipline focuses on specific aspects and scale of time. Figure 1.1 gives an idea of the general focus of time in some selected disciplines. While science and religion bicker about the beginning of time, neuroscience is focusing on the moment-to-moment mechanisms of the *time-less* gene in governing the circadian rhythm. And whereas the range of time in experimental psychology is typically no more than a few minutes, the basic units of time for geologic time includes millennia and eons. A thorough discourse on time, no pun intended, can take an eternity.

Human-computer interaction generally involves time units from milliseconds (such as instantaneous response time) to hours (such as installing an operating system), although other interactions can go well beyond a few hours. Scheduling weekly maintenance tasks in a calendar application can easily involve weeks and months. Some complex mathematical computations can take multiple computers days to weeks to complete. This book focuses on the experience of time in day-to-day and observable human-computer interactions.

---

[2] Franciscus Cornelis Donders (1818-1889) basically argued that the time taken to make a decision increases linearly as a function of the number of choices. Simply put, the more choices there are, the more time is taken to make the right decision. This was replicated by many researchers, most notably E. Hicks in 1952, whose work led to the formulation of the Hick-Hyman Law.

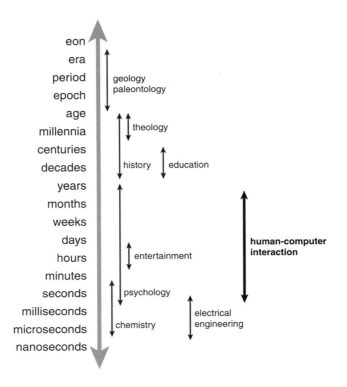

FIGURE 1.1

A relative representation and comparison of the time scales of selected disciplines

Can Time Be Engineered?

Pairing up the terms *engineering* and *time* inevitably conjures up images from H. G. Wells's *Time Machine*: a clunky machine made up of flickering tungsten light bulbs, countless spinning cogwheels of all sizes, and a bucket seat. This represents Hollywood's idea of time engineering, and, as far as we know, at the time of writing there is no time-travel vehicle or mechanism. We are certain that time can't really be accelerated or decelerated. Right?

Well…while time is *objectively* measured, it is *subjectively* experienced. Two individuals may experience a three-hour documentary differently, depending on each individual's interests, context, or language, for instance. Although we can't roll back the clock to see how the Egyptians built the Great Pyramid of Giza or accelerate time to celebrate the birthdays of our great-great grandchildren, we can deal with the way we *experience* time.

The key to engineering subjective time is to engineer the factors that affect the experience of time.

Apart from gravitational time dilation,[3] the loss of consciousness, rare neurological diseases, psychotropic substances, and other similar factors, ordinary and simple experiences in life can affect the way we experience time. A seemingly innocuous typo or wording in the UI, for instance, is enough to cause users to experience time—for better or worse—quite differently. Figure 1.2 shows two exaggerated examples.

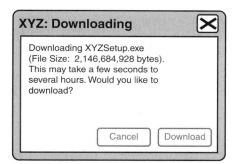 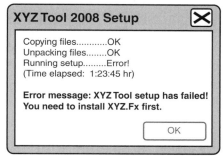

FIGURE 1.2

Examples of how seemingly innocuous wording in the UI (left dialog) or design (right dialog) can result in a less-than-optimal experience for the user

Why Design and Engineer Time?

Before delving into the reasons why we should design and engineer time to optimize human-computer interaction, consider this: In some instances, we might not need to bother dealing with time and timing issues in the products we make. For many tools and solutions not intended for personal use and not intended for sale or use by others, certain aspects of the product might not necessarily be of top priority. These are the duct-tape and coat-hanger solutions that are designed for practicality and utility, not elegance and performance. Examples include hobby projects, personalized Excel macros, and partially functioning prototypes of applications.

---

[3] Gravitational time dilation is one of two of Einstein's theories on how *objective* time can be altered. Einstein's predictions were confirmed by the famous Pound-Rebka experiment in 1959 and the Hafele-Keating experiment in 1971. Theoretically, suppose one embarks on a vehicle that travels at nearly the speed of light and takes a trip for a year. According to Einstein's theory, the passenger would return to discover that his children are not one but seven years older!

Another possible instance when timing issues aren't (but should really be) top priority is when the solutions are developed or customized for internal use in a company. Overall usability for such homespun solutions typically goes out the window. In an international study on intranet usability, for example, the Nielsen Norman Group found several glaring usability issues with such tools. If these were corrected, the consultants estimate that it would save an average mid-size company about $5 million in employee productivity. Why many homespun internal solutions do not make the grade could be due to many factors but chief among them is a *training-usability tradeoff* (see Figure 1.3). That is, it is commonly expected for an employee to learn or be trained to use the internal solution as part of his or her job responsibility, so usability issues, such as ease of use or discoverability, aren't high on the priority list. In contrast, for many commercial solutions, it is unreasonable to require extensive training, so more attention is paid to making the solution more usable.

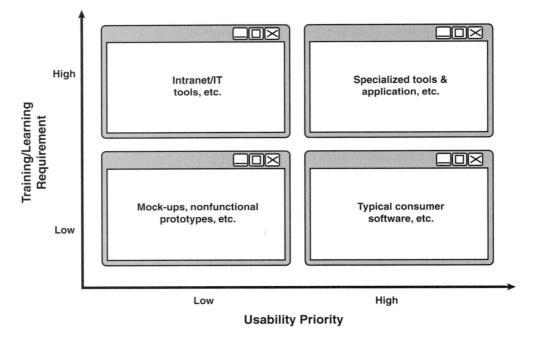

FIGURE 1.3

Tools designed for internal use in a company (upper-left corner) typically tend to receive little usability attention because there is some expectation that the users of the tools will learn or be trained to use the tool. Commercial applications, such as a CD-burning application, would ideally be in the lower-right corner, where little training is required as a result of a relatively higher usability focus. Exceptions fall into the top upper-right and lower-left corners.

In most other cases, ensuring an optimal computing experience from a time perception perspective will matter because all software products inherently require users to expend time: installing, searching, downloading, compiling, file transferring, and so on. Some of these interactions require short amounts of time, but others are "time guzzlers," taking hours to successfully complete. There are other compelling and specific reasons why everyone who makes any commercial or noncommercial solution should pay attention to how it expends users' time.

Unlike Money, Time Is Variable

We all know that *time is money*,[4] but what we don't always know is that we are not very good at budgeting time. Recent studies have shown that people overcommit themselves to future assignments and tasks because they think that they will have a surplus of time to fulfill the commitments. In the researchers' words, this is when "Yes!" turns into "Damn!" Even for shorter durations, as we discuss in the next chapter, our perception of time is highly susceptible to distortion.

Time and money are undoubtedly the top two commodities for people. However, unlike money, time is a commodity that fluctuates in its value depending on many factors, such as time of day and context. Consumer research has found that different hours during the day are valued differently. For instance, some people are less patient during lunch time, so every minute during lunch time is more precious than the minute that goes by during a sluggish afternoon. Even within the same window of time, the value of time can be weighed differently in different contexts. For example, research shows that people value waiting time three times more than in-vehicle travel time, which may explain why some of us will favor taking an alternate country road over inching along the highway to get to our destinations, even if both routes take the same amount of time.

Perception Drives Everything

There should be little doubt that perception of performance drives satisfaction. We all want faster downloads, quicker results, more responsive interfaces, and so on. Many lines of research in various disciplines have repeatedly shown that what is perceived is more important than what is objectively presented because perception drives behavior and decisions. Figure 1.4 shows a model (Technology Acceptance Model or TAM) that relates, among other factors, perceived usefulness and perceived ease of use to eventual actual acceptance and sustained use of a technology. In fact, altering perception to simulate

---

[4] An economics professor from England actually derived a mathematical formula to calculate the actual monetary cost of time for an individual.

reality is the basis of many forms of artistic expressions and entertainment. Many other factors also drive satisfaction, such as usability, aesthetics, and affordability. What glues these factors to satisfaction is perception. No matter how fast we make a download, how usable we design a product, how pretty we make the presentation layer, and how reasonable a price we set, if perception is distorted at any point, all bets are off.

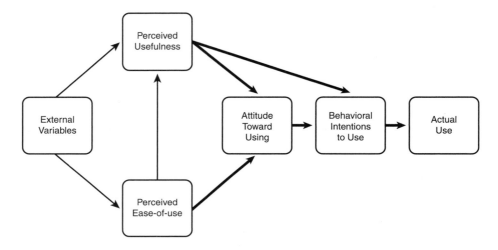

FIGURE 1.4

The Technology Acceptance Model (TAM) by Fred Davis shows the importance of perception in predicting the adoption and use of a technology.

As for the perception of performance, consumer research has repeatedly confirmed a simple fact: When performance is perceived to be better than expectation, satisfaction is high. Conversely, when performance is perceived to be below expectation, satisfaction is low. This maxim is known as *Maister's First Law of Service,* which basically states that satisfaction is a function of *disconfirmation,* or the difference between what was perceived and what was expected. Simply put, when perception falls short of what was expected, dissatisfaction rises.

Who Is the Time Engineer?

So time can be engineered, but who is the time engineer? The store employee at Costco who prescans your merchandise to expedite your checkout process while you stand in line is a time engineer. The clinic clerk who makes you fill out the lengthy but necessary paperwork while you wait for the doctor is a time engineer. The theme park technician who installs the interesting novelties along the waiting lines of popular rides is a time engineer. The common factors in each of these examples should be evident. In each case, a practice or modification to a situation resulted in a more expeditious experience for the customer, the patient, and the patrons. Thus, a time engineer is one who applies principles of time perception and techniques to an existing solution to achieve an optimal experience for people who interact with the solution.

About This Book

Organization of Chapters

The overall goal of this book is to consolidate knowledge, research, and practice and make them coherent enough to be applied to practical problems that you may encounter when developing solutions. To accomplish this, after this chapter, this book has been roughly divided into two parts. The first part consists of the following eight chapters. These chapters cover specific topics in dealing with time and timing in the UI.

CHAPTER 2, "PERCEPTION AND TOLERANCE"

This chapter discusses the importance of differentiating between *perceived durations* and *actual durations,* and the role of *user tolerance* and the factors that influence it.

CHAPTER 3, "USER AND SYSTEM RESPONSE TIMES"

This chapter introduces both user and system response times and discusses industry standards on maximum acceptable response times.

CHAPTER 4, "RESPONSIVENESS"

This chapter defines responsiveness as a function of what users expect and introduces four responsiveness classes: instantaneous, immediate, continuous, and captive.

CHAPTER 5, "DETECTING TIMING DIFFERENCES"

This chapter introduces the basic concepts in human detection of timing changes to help define performance objectives, such as setting performance goals or determining regression allowance.

CHAPTER 6, "PROGRESS INDICATION"

This chapter introduces a way to classify progress indications and explain how these classes can help you determine the most suitable type of indication to use.

CHAPTER 7, "EXPRESSING TIME"

This chapter discusses when and how you should express time in your product and introduces the use of time anchors.

CHAPTER 8, "USER FLOW"

This chapter discusses how to ensure an optimal user flow using concepts borrowed from research in the psychology of flow.

CHAPTER 9, "TESTING TIME"

This chapter talks about various approaches to collecting data for actual duration, perceived duration, or user tolerance.

Many problems, limitations, and obstacles that you will encounter in developing your solution can be solved by overhauling the underlying architecture, upgrading the hardware, or adding more horsepower. Unfortunately, these approaches are frequently costly in effort, time, and money.

The second part consists of the last two chapters, which present some alternatives to the expensive solutions:

CHAPTER 10, "TECHNIQUES"

This chapter describes some perception management and tolerance management techniques that can be considered in the design of UIs.

CHAPTER 11, "VIOLATIONS"

This chapter describes some of these violations and discusses some ways to prevent and correct these violations.

Vocabulary

The concepts and practices mentioned in this book are meant to be general. That is, they are not only applicable just to specific software applications running in specific operating system or specific computer systems. To that end, I have attempted to use general terms to reflect the general applicability and scope of this book.

SOLUTION

The term *solution* is used in this book to cover software applications, services, websites, devices, hardware, and any other product that involves some UI that is sending, receiving, or exchanging some information with the user. Examples include an e-commerce website, an antivirus software program, a CBT (computer-based training) tutorial program, and a simple e-mail program.

PROCESS

In the context of this book, the term *process* refers to an operation, task, function, or any activity (or a set of these activities) that is carried out by the solution. Typically, one or more time-related aspects of the solution, such as the start time, duration, and completion time, are meaningful to the user. Some examples of process include those with relatively long durations, such as installation, data download, database queries, and those with relatively short durations, such as behaviors of UI controls, zooming, and resizing of windows.

USER

The term *user* refers to the end user, consumer, operator, or any individual who is directly or indirectly interacting with your solution. Beyond the obvious user who sits in front of a computer screen or a laptop, these may also be the bank customers who are interacting with the software installed in the ATM, the deliveryman who is using a handheld device to manage deliveries, or the nurse who is using sophisticated medical equipment to monitor the health of a patient.

Painting a Thousand Words

To help better express the theory and the practice, the pain and the bliss, and the techniques and violations, I have included nearly 100 diagrams throughout this book. Many of these diagrams feature UIs from the products of one of two fictitious brands: ABC and XYZ. The UIs found in ABC's suite of solutions illustrate examples of good design and practices that lead to a good user experience. The solutions by XYZ, on the other hand, contain UI faux pas and design blunders that should be avoided.

Going Down the Rabbit Hole

Throughout the book, you will find a wide spectrum of knowledge from psychological theories with pedantic names to commonsense knowledge, from Nobel-caliber research of eminent scientists to dissertation projects of fledgling graduate students, and from textbook techniques practiced by usability professionals to effective practices used by the store clerk. This book leans toward the practical and the applicable. In case you want to go further down the rabbit hole, I have provided a list of research, suggested readings, and literature at the end of each chapter. The list for each topic has been kept short to prevent the rabbit hole from becoming a full-blown bibliographical index. In all likelihood, following one resource will lead you to more resources—thus the function of the rabbit hole! Most of these resources will support what is visited in the chapter, but some will, as it always will be, present contradictory theories, counterarguments, or alternative approaches. It is then the reader's challenge to consider all the knowledge and facts, factor in the context of the problem at hand, and make a final decision on how to approach fixing the problem.

Rabbit Hole

Classic Psychological Experiments Involving Time

Donders, F. C. (1868). Die Schnelligkeit psychischer Processe ("On the speed of mental processes") *Archiv für Anatomie und Physiologie und wissenschaftliche Medizin,* 657–681.

Ebbinghaus, H. (1885). *Über das Gedächtnis: Untersuchungen zur experimentellen Psychologie.* Leipzig: Duncker and Humblot. Trans. (1913) H. A. Ruger and C. E. Bussenius, *Memory: A Contribution to Experimental Psychology.* New York: Teachers College, Columbia University. Reprint (1964). New York: Dover.

Seminal Papers on Time Perception

Allan, L. G. (1979). The perception of time. *Perception & Psychophysics,* 26, 340–354.

Fraisse, P. (1963). *The Psychology of Time.* New York: Harper & Row.

James, W. (1890). *Principles of Psychology.* New York: Holt. (Author's note: Online version at http://psychclassics.yorku.ca/James/Principles/. Read Chapter 15.)

Woodrow, H. (1951). Time perception. In *Handbook of Experimental Psychology* (Ed) S. S. Stevens. New York: Wiley.

Scientific Study and Manipulation of Objective Time

Hafele, J. and R. Keating (1972). Around the world atomic clocks: Predicted relativistic time gains. *Science,* 177, 166–170.

Pound, R. V. and G. A. Rebka, Jr. (1959). Gravitational red-shift in nuclear resonance. *Physical Review Letters,* 3, 439–441.

Books on Time

Hawking, S. (1988). *A Brief History of Time.* Bantam Books.

McCready, S. (2001). *The Discovery of Time.* Naperville, IL: Sourcebooks, Inc.

Whitrow, G. J. (1972). *What Is Time? The classic account of the nature of time.* New York: Oxford Press. (Author's note: See "The Literature of Time," starting on page 142, for a substantially more comprehensive list of literature on the topic.)

Time and Money

Leclerc, F., B. H. Schmitt, and L. Dube (1995). Waiting time and decision making: Is time like money? *Journal of Consumer Research,* 22, 110–119.

"Time is Money, Professor Proves." CNN.com/SCI-TECH. May 29, 2002. (Author's note: Online at http://archives.cnn.com/2002/TECH/science/05/29/time.money/.)

Zauberman, G. and J. G. Lynch (2005). Resource slack and propensity to discount delayed investments of time versus money. *Journal of Experimental Psychology: General,* 134, 23–37.

Time Perception and Productivity

Barber, R. E. and H. C. Lucas (1983). System response time, operator productivity, and job satisfaction. *Communications of the ACM,* 26, 972–996.

Miller, R. B. (1968). Response time in man-computer conversational transaction. Fall Joint Comp. Conf. U.S.A., 267–277.

Shneiderman, B. (1984). Response time and display rate in human performance with computers. *Computing Survey,* 16, 265–285.

Time Perception and Satisfaction

Davis, M. M. and J. Heineke (1998). How disconfirmation, perception and actual waiting times impact customer satisfaction. *International Journal of Service Industry Management,* 9, 64–73.

Davis, M. M. and T. E. Vollman (1990). A framework for relating waiting time and customer satisfaction in a service operation. *The Journal of Services Marketing,* 4, 61–69.

Durrande-Moreau, A. (1999). Waiting for service: Ten years of empirical research. *International Journal of Service Industry Management,* 10, 171–189.

Maister, D. H. (1985). The psychology of waiting lines. In Czepiel (Ed.), *The Service Encounter.* Lexington, MA: Lexington Books. 113–123.

Tom, G. and S. Lucey (1995). Waiting time delays and customer satisfaction in supermarkets. *Journal of Services Marketing,* 9, 20–29.

Time Perception and Software Use

Davis, F. D. (1989). Perceived usefulness, perceived ease of use, and user acceptance of information technology. *MIS Quarterly,* 13, 319–340.

Morris, M. G. and A. Dillon (1997). How user perceptions influence software use. *IEEE Software,* 14, 58–65.

Rabbit Holes

Carroll, L., (2000). *Alice's Adventures in Wonderland and Through the Looking Glass.* New York: Penguin Group. (Author's note: This is where the *rabbit hole* term comes from. Online at http://www.gutenberg.org/etext/11.)

2

Perception and Tolerance

Beyond actual and objective timing, it is also important to consider what users perceive and how much they are willing to tolerate. For example, a three-minute download can feel like five minutes, but users may only be willing to tolerate one minute. This chapter discusses the importance of differentiating between *perceived durations* and *actual durations* and describes the role of *user tolerance*.

ption and Tolerance

Your users are complaining that some process in your solution is unacceptably slow. You run a performance test and determine that everything is performing as specified. Nevertheless, you obligingly spend several days to tweak your solution and make the process a little faster. You optimistically release a new and improved version of your solution. A few weeks later, the verdict is in…still unacceptably slow.

Reviewers from a reputable computer magazine ran a survey to compare your solution and a competitor's solution. For responsiveness, users gave the competitor's solution five out of five stars and gave your solution two measly stars. Incredulous, you put both solutions to a responsiveness test. Result: Both solutions were equally responsive. What is going on?

Mainstream computer users typically do not time their interactions in day-to-day tasks and are more likely to ignore timing unless it comes to their attention, particularly when the delays are unusually longer than normal. When users do gauge durations, they are more likely to rely on mental estimations rather than objective measurements. Because perception is highly susceptible to distortion, what users perceive may be quite different from what is actual.

Consider the following questions:

- How can we make the download faster?
- How can we make the download appear faster?
- How do we make users tolerate the download?

Although these appear to be the same, they are really different questions that require different answers. Depending on the context, limitations, and other constraints, one question may be more suitable to ask and to answer than the others. The answer to the first question will likely be a purely technical one that alters the actual process, protocol, or operation of how things are done. Such approaches, borrowing from the service and retail industry, can be described as *operational*. In the service and retail industry, *operational management* involves substantial changes to the way business is conducted. Back to the first question, if time and resources permit the implementation of new technologies to make the download faster (such as using better compression algorithms, boosting hardware, etc.), it is a good question to ask and answer.

Whereas the answer to the first question will typically call for a revamp or an overhaul, the answer to the second is best related to a makeover because it employs an approach without making drastic operational changes. In the software engineering context, when there are technical limitations, this second question is a better question to ask and answer. Providing distraction to divert people's attention from a long wait is a prime example. Such techniques fall under what is termed *perception management* in retail and other service industries. For example, a bank manager may choose to employ more staff to reduce wait time (operations management) or install a television set along the waiting lines (perceptual management).

Lastly, there will be circumstances when operational limitations (budget constraints, unavailability of hardware, schedule, etc.) and delays are too difficult to "disguise," such as complex searches that yield large results that necessarily take time to complete. In such instances, it becomes critical to focus on increasing *user tolerance*. Such situations make the last question most appropriate. *Tolerance management* doesn't attempt to "disguise" the actual duration, but rather, it focuses on making users more tolerant and patient of inevitable waits or delays. Figure 2.1 provides a flowchart that summarizes the approaches to these management practices and shows when each should be applied. More perceptual and tolerance techniques, as well as violations, are found in Chapters 10, "Techniques," and 11, "Violations."

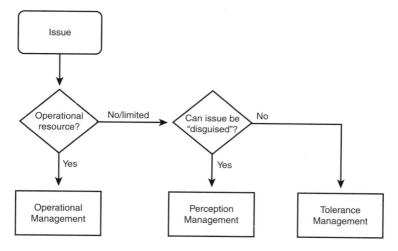

FIGURE 2.1

A flowchart that simplifies and generalizes when operational, perception, and tolerance management ought to be considered

Real or Perceived?

A complaint about the performance of a solution, such as the example at the beginning of this chapter, is similar to a complaint of slow service in a restaurant in that the complaints may be *real* or *perceived*: Do they *know* that it was slow or did they *feel* that it was slow? The diner may be getting antsy because the waiter has indeed forgotten to pass the diner's order to the cook, or the diner noticed that another table has been served ahead of his. Likewise in the computing context, the user may be detecting some slack because of a variety of reasons. A download may indeed be slow because there is an unusually high amount of network traffic, or it may be perceived as slow because the user needs the information urgently.

As a relevant side note, establishing the distinction between what is real and what is perceived is important, but what users report should not be contested. If you have to verify with the user whether a reported duration is actual or perceived, some care should be taken. That is, it would be better to ask, "Can you give me more information about the delay?" than to ask the seemingly innocuous, "Did you actually time the performance?"

Reality: Actual Time

Although this book focuses on perception and tolerance management, there are several important considerations as far as objective timing is concerned. First, in a human-computer interaction context, objective timing, such as response time, must be defined in the user's world. Second, objective timing must be obtained via objective means. Last, collecting as much data as possible is always good. We discuss the first consideration in the next chapter. Let's take a closer look at the last two considerations.

Precision: Objective Time from Objective Measures

It is critical to establish reliable and valid actual durations because it is the only objective metric you have in investigating user-reported time and timing-related issues. Establishing a reliable and valid data will be critical when you compare it against perceived duration. There are many ways to determine the actual durations. Sometimes these numbers may be obtained from informal measurements, time-stamped logs, technical specifications, or derived from formulaic or programmatic calculations. In all cases, because actual durations reflect *objective* time, it must be measured by *objective* means. We postpone a more thorough discussion on this to Chapter 9, "Testing Time."

When actual durations are reported by a secondary source (that is, not measured directly by you), such as the user or some documentation, it is a good practice for you to verify how the numbers were obtained and attempt to reproduce the same numbers. Vague estimations are not adequate substitutes for actual duration. If the process was not objectively measured, it is more appropriately looked at as a perceived duration.

Data: Volume, Variability, Variety

Besides precision, volume of data is critical, too. Whenever possible, multiple measurements of the duration in question ought to be obtained from a variety of methods of measurement to establish and analyze for meaningful patterns. For example, in-depth data analysis, such as a time-series analysis, can reveal suggestive trends, such as a bottleneck effect that causes the duration to lengthen each time the process is started or engaged. Similarly, simply plotting the frequency distribution of the data can reveal where the data is centered and how the data is spread out, which might help diagnose the problem. Figure 2.2 shows some hypothetical objective data showing the response latency in the loading of a website before and after the implementation of new software. Such an analysis would not be possible without collecting lots of data.

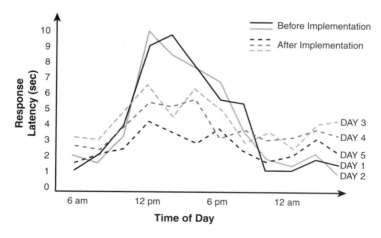

FIGURE 2.2

Hypothetical objective data showing the response latency in the loading of a website before (solid lines) and after (dotted lines) the implementation of new software. Collecting lots of data allows for more revealing analyses.

Perception: Psychological Time

While objective reality concerns facts (whether we sense it or not), perception concerns how we experience objective reality (whether it is factual or not). We go about our lives every day with our mind loaded with ideas and theories about how and why things are the way they are. Whether we are accurate in our perception of these everyday events is typically unimportant. By and large, we don't question our perception. Likewise, when someone perceives that some event took "about an hour," that's how long it took in that perceiver's mind (see Figure 2.3). A useful way to think about perceived duration is to imagine the perceiver as a stopwatch that reports the duration, albeit imprecise, of some event. This is referred to many in psychology as the *psychological time.*

FIGURE 2.3

Perceived duration should never be assumed to be true and accurate to the actual objective duration.

Subjectivity: Do You See What I See?

In the strictest sense, perception concerns what the brain does with the information it receives from the senses. Suppose a five-pointed star is presented to an individual (see Figure 2.4). The visual stimulus reaches the eye, and tiny photoreceptors in the retina detect and convert the visual information into neural signals that will then be routed to the various regions of the brain for processing. At and beyond this point, many factors, such as age, education, culture, and even beliefs and practices, will determine what the symbol means to the individual. In the mind of a first grader, the symbol is perceived as a symbol of reward for a job well done. In the mind of a Wiccan, the symbol will likely represent aspects of pagan faith. In the mind of a diner, the symbol could very well indicate the spiciness of the dish! In the mind of a soldier, the symbol might designate an officer's rank. As such, what is sensed in the physical world should never be assumed to be true and accurate to what is perceived in the mind of the perceiver.

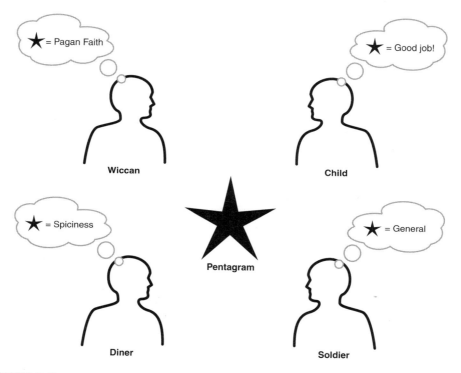

FIGURE 2.4

Perception is what the brain does with the information it receives from the sense. A five-pointed star may represent the pagan faith, indicate the degree of spiciness of a dish, express a job well done, or symbolize the rank of a general.

Distortion: Do Not Trust Your Brain

A common but wrong assumption is that what we recall from memory is reliable and infallible. Years of memory research have shown us that our memory is not entirely reliable. Memories of time and timing, just like any other information we can hold in memory, are not impervious to distortion. Memory is typically viewed as a three-stage process—encoding, storage, and retrieval—and at each stage, information is susceptible to distortion (see Figure 2.5). During the encoding, physical constraints or physiological limitations (for example, short-sightedness) can cause the event to be witnessed inaccurately. During storage, remembered information is susceptible to forgetting (or decay as memory researchers call it) over time as well as other distortions. For the retrieval of remembered information, the work of E. Loftus has shown that people's recollections and reporting of remembered events are highly susceptible to subtle influences, such as the wording of the question used to cue for the recollection.[1]

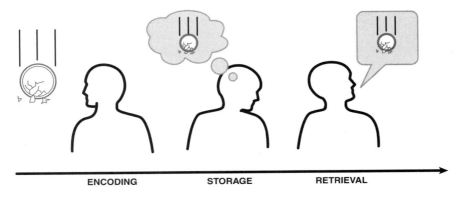

ENCODING   **STORAGE**   **RETRIEVAL**

FIGURE 2.5

Memory is commonly viewed in three stages: encoding, storage, and retrieval. At each stage, information about what is experienced is susceptible to distortion.

There are as many types of time distortions as the types of questions you typically ask about time: *duration* (how long something took), *occurrence* (when something occurred), and *order* (what happened first, etc.). Order involves two or more occurrences in time, and an occurrence (such as when something started or ended) is, in essence, a type of duration because you are really comparing the elapsed time or remaining time between the occurrence and another meaningful point in time. Consider the following questions: When did the computer shut down? When will the beta application be released? Although they appear as questions about a single point in time, the answer to each

---

[1] In her classic memory experiment, Loftus showed students a film of an automobile accident and later asked them to estimate the speeds of the cars involved. Estimations of the speed of the cars differed depending on the way the question was asked. For the group that was asked "About how fast were the cars going when they hit each other?" the average estimated speed was 34 mph. For the group that was asked "About how fast were the cars going when they smashed each other?" the estimate was 40.5 mph.

question necessarily involves comparison to another point in time, typically the present. Whenever two points in time are compared, you are really dealing with duration. Durations can only take two forms of distortion: *overestimation* and *underestimation*.

Tolerance: Valued Time

Research shows that when people are asked to recall the duration of a recent activity, short durations tend to be overestimated, whereas long durations tend to be underestimated. This is known in human timing literature as *Vierordt's Law*. However, most problematic time-related experiences don't arise when users are actively performing a task or engaging the user interface (UI). The majority of time-related issues have to do with instances when users are not able to perform their task or continue interacting with the computer. This is, of course, more commonly but painfully known as *waiting*. Research shows that three in four people tend to overestimate waiting times and that such overestimations can be as high as 25% of the actual time.

But what is long and short? What is considered slow and fast? Why is the same ten seconds blazingly fast for one person but irritatingly slow for another?

Quantity Versus Quality

As mentioned in Chapter 1, "Designing and Engineering Time," the value of time fluctuates and varies according to many factors. A ten-minute wait for a person who is already 15 minutes late for an important meeting is excruciating. The same ten-minute wait for a person who has already waited three days for a package to arrive is trivial. Tolerance for any given duration, therefore, comes from the subjective value that the duration is given. In many ways, the mind and the stopwatch are alike in that they function like clocks, but it is important to remember that a clock merely reports timing and doesn't make a judgment of speed or satisfaction. That is, perceived duration is strictly a *quantitative* assessment and ought to be void of all other forms of *qualitative* assessment. Whereas, perceived durations yield a quantitative value ("The installation took an hour…"), tolerance is determined by the qualitative value ("That is too slow because it should only take 15 minutes!").

The Mental Benchmark

The picture is incomplete without tying perceived durations back to tolerance. Remember that mainstream users typically do not deliberately clock operations and processes in the computer products they use, but they are keenly attuned to real or perceived delays. (There is, of course, a subset of users who will assess performance for a variety of reasons and will therefore have objective measurements.) In either case, a common factor can be found in both subsets: All durations are meaningless without a reference for comparison. For example, merely stating that the tennis ball is $2\frac{1}{2}$ inches in diameter is factual, quantitative, and descriptive but devoid of any other meaning. If I were to add that because the ball is $2\frac{1}{2}$ inches wide, I cannot use a chain-link fence with a mesh size of 3 inches to surround the tennis court, then knowing the diameter becomes meaningful.

Similarly, some form of a benchmark is needed for an actual duration to be meaningful. This is no different for perceived duration: Without some reference, such as prior or similar experiences, perception will be meaningless. In fact, quantitative models of animal timing contain a component representing reference memory. One such model, formulated by Gibbon, Church, and Meck, is shown in Figure 2.6. In the computing context, when a user states that something is slow or fast, you can always count on the current perception being matched to something in memory, such as prior experiences, expectations, and so forth. These perceptual benchmarks enable the user to decide how to characterize the perceived duration. For example, if a user remembers that a specific software application typically fully loads in about five seconds, and on one occasion, the application took twice as much time to launch, the user detects the difference and suspects that something is amiss.

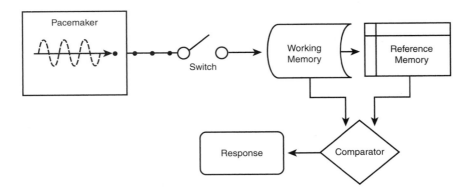

FIGURE 2.6

Many models of timing, such as this one by Gibbon, Church, and Meck, include a component that represents a reference memory that holds a remembered duration. In this model, the reference memory is compared against what is perceived in real time in working memory, and a response is made based on outcome of the comparison.

What is established in memory as an expectation will set a *tolerance threshold,* beyond which perceived durations will be judged as slow. Conversely, if perceived duration is experienced beneath the threshold, it will be judged as fast (see Figure 2.7). Unlike the comparison between actual and perceived durations, this concerns how the user *feels* about the duration relative to what he or she thinks and knows. This concept of tolerance threshold is similar to the idea of the *threshold of indignation* mentioned by P. Saffo in *Bringing Design to Software.* You can reasonably consider the former a timing variant of the latter, which is defined by Saffo as the "maximal behavioral compromise that we are willing to make to get a task done."

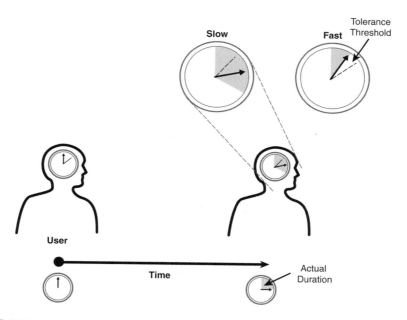

FIGURE 2.7

Perceived duration is only meaningful when it is compared to a tolerance threshold. If the perceived duration is shorter than the tolerance threshold, the user interprets that as fast. Conversely, if the duration is perceived as longer than the tolerance threshold, the user interprets the duration as slow.

Time-Related Factors Affecting Tolerance

The obvious factors that influence tolerance are the ones that have a temporal dimension—that is, the ones that have some explicit timing metric. Because most of these factors are relatively obvious, they are fairly easy to determine with a little probing, measurement, or research.

USAGE AND EXPERIENCE

Although mainstream users do not typically keep explicit timing on how fast the computer is in performing particular tasks, memory of durations established through repeated usage and experience can be, although not exactly accurate, quite reliable for practical purposes. Take booting a computer, for instance. It is not uncommon for users to press the power button to start the computer, walk away to attend to other tasks, and then return after a period of time confidently believing the computer is ready. Because such tasks are performed frequently, longer-than-usual delays in booting (for example, after a hardware upgrade, booting another computer with the same configuration) will begin to reduce tolerance. On the other extreme, a lack of usage or experience may adversely affect tolerance, too.

STANDARDS AND BENCHMARKS

When particular durations fall short of published or posted metrics, the tolerance threshold will, obviously, be negatively affected. A more important point to consider is that these metrics can be established by *any* source, and for the average user, the credibility of these numbers pivots more on general popularity than science or engineering. For example, if a popular source (say, *Wired* magazine) reports that research shows that most good websites fully load in less than two seconds, chances are that number will become the de facto standard for many readers. Whether the metric is empirically established is typically not challenged by mainstream users. As such, it becomes very important to identify what these standards or benchmarks are, how they are determined, how a product or service in question matches up to them, and, if necessary, what corrective measures one can take.

COMPARATIVE REFERENCES

As mentioned in an earlier section, users cannot express whether something is fast or slow unless they are evaluating it against a point of comparative reference. For most users, the comparative reference will most likely be the same feature between versions or variants (such as a Web-based version and a desktop version) of the product, a different feature within the same product, the same feature of another product, or different feature of another product. Table 2.1 shows some examples. Establishing what users are using as a comparative reference can be done through a variety of means (focus group, observations, interviews, etc.), but the main objective is to be aware of what these comparative references are, and then, if necessary, provide countermeasures if users are evaluating a feature, service, or product "unfairly" against an *incomparable* comparative reference.

Table 2.1 Common Examples of Comparative Reference

	Same Product or Service	Comparable Product or Service
Same feature or function	Adding Favorites in Internet Explorer 6 versus Adding Favorites in Internet Explorer 7	Performing an Internet search on Google versus Performing an Internet search on Yahoo!
Different but comparable feature or function	Copying and pasting text into a document versus Copying and pasting an image into a document	Watching video streamed over the Internet versus Watching video from a downloaded video file

INDICATIONS ON USER INTERFACE

Sometimes users lose tolerance and patience simply because an explicit promise of how long something will last is broken. For example, the UI is indicating that a particular process will take under five minutes, but seven minutes have already elapsed. Besides textual information, users also use indications from progress bars to gauge how long something will last. When the duration exceeds what is indicated or suggested, tolerance quickly diminishes. Whereas the lack of information causes people to be impatient, explicit information that turns out to be inaccurate has similar adverse effects on users' tolerance.

Nontime-Related Factors Affecting Tolerance

By far, the factors that influence tolerance are nontemporal. That is, they do not contain any timing metric, but they regulate how much waiting time users are willing to tolerate. In comparison to factors mentioned in the previous section, these factors, which can be comfortably labeled context, are less objective but are nevertheless important to consider when assessing users' tolerance.

ATTEMPTS, REPEATED FAILURES

Most users do not give up on the first failure of some tasks, in that they are willing to tolerate occasional system hiccups and repeat a few attempts to perform a task. Take surfing on the Internet as a prime example. Users typically will not throw their hands in the air and give up when the browser immediately reports a 404 page loading error. Chances are they will reopen the browser, retype the URL, or click the Refresh or Reload button. Had users been intolerant of system hiccups, they would have immediately closed the browser and claimed that the product is defective or has malfunctioned upon encountering the very first 404 error. Because mainstream computer users are tolerant and adaptive, software makers can get away with including the Refresh or Reload button on Internet browsers, and hardware makers can get away with Reset buttons!

There is a caveat, however. This unique "user clemency" appears to hinge on at least two factors. The first concerns the perceived reliability and stability of the product. Some products are perceived and expected to be highly reliable and stable, so including a button or function that resets the product would be odd. A television set, for example, does not come with a reset or refresh button for the end user because it is regarded as an appliance that just works. Likewise, certain computer products are perceived to be more stable and reliable than others, which means they are expected to be less prone to hiccups. For example, users will be more tolerant of hiccups while reaching a Web page than when using a word processor to type a memo. Users of beta programs, too, are more tolerant of application glitches in the beta product than glitches in a released product. As such, user clemency varies as a function of perceived stability, in that users are more forgiving of processes that are understandably less stable.

The second factor that appears to influence user clemency is the user's perceived certainty about why something is not working. For example, users are more tolerant if their newly purchased mobile device doesn't synchronize with their PC right away because the user will likely think that there could be many reasons why the synchronization failed: device not configured, Bluetooth not enabled, software not installed on PC, and so on. However, armed with some certainties (Bluetooth is enabled because a blue indicator light is blinking, the software successfully installed on the PC according to the instructions, or it has been working ever since it was set it up a month ago, etc.), tolerance for failures will quickly diminish over repeated failed attempts because each trial and error narrows down the fault of the failure to the device or application.

TIME OF THE DAY, DAY OF THE WEEK

For many modern and industrial societies, time of the day and day of the week (and perhaps even month of the year) may play a critical role in regulating the users' tolerance. Research has shown, for example, that many fast food restaurant customers are more impatient during lunch time than dinner time. In this instance, time constraints of lunch time (for example, having to return to work) obviously play a primary role. Day of the week can also play a significant role in tolerance, too, as well hinted by the phrase *Monday blues*. It is reasonable to speculate that many office workers will have certain priorities upon returning to the office at the beginning of the week. For many who manage their appointments and tasks on the computer (such as scheduling and managing meetings in the calendar feature of their e-mail application, or keeping track of work or purchase orders in an internal application), accessing this information may be of top priority at the beginning of the week, and therefore tolerance will be low to begin with because the desire to obtain the information quickly is higher. If the application goes through a series of processes (as it does each time it loads up) that delays the user from getting to the information (or worse, suggests to the user that it is time to perform some indeterminate maintenance), tolerance will decrease each tick of the second. As such, the perceived urgency and priority of the task at hand will alter the tolerance threshold.

EMOTIVE STATES

Research has repeatedly shown that under significant emotive or stressful circumstances, perception is highly susceptible to distortion. For instance, some software products are built to be used in environments that are necessarily more stressful than others. For example, using a word processor to type a term paper and using a touch-screen POS (point of sale) system at a restaurant during peak hours are two very different experiences for a college student who works part time at the restaurant. Likewise, searching on the Internet for the latest celebrity gossip and retrieving information in a police squad car about a suspicious driver are likewise experienced very differently by the same police officer who likes to keep on top of Hollywood news. Therefore, it pays to scope out the usage scenarios of a product or service and determine whether any modifications ought to be made to accommodate the user experience. An application designed for the presentation of information, for example, should be optimized to launch promptly without tedious and unnecessary steps. An information-retrieval application, such as the one installed in the laptops in police cars, ought to help the police officer get to the relevant and accurate information quickly without the hassle of meaningless dialogs and queries.

BIAS

For a variety of reasons, a user may have little tolerance for a process no matter how optimized it is. Disgruntled office workers who were informed by corporate that a new Web-based Internet application has replaced the current client-based application (which everyone has gotten used to) may naturally be less tolerant of the new implementation—the typical "I hate this new system" reaction. Reputation and brand names of some products may also cause users to be biased. Sometimes, the reputation of the product may have preceded it, such as in reviews, consumer reports, or word of mouth. Other times, it could be the classic guilt by association, where products made by the same maker are preconceived to be under par. In such cases, some users may seek to amplify the faults and limitations of the product to lend support to their preconception. On the flip side, the opposite effect is the *Halo Effect,* where users assume that the product has some desirable quality and caliber because it carries the same brand name as another favored product.

CULTURE, TRENDS, FADS

While bias works at the individual user level, factors that work on a much larger scale can affect the tolerance of the individual. More specifically, trends and fads can play an influential role in building tolerance for a product. The same complaints for a product (difficult to use, bulky, too small, too big, too slow, etc.) can quickly become moot when society or peers declare that the same product is the "in" thing to have or use. A prime example is the failed adoption of Newton, one of the earliest PDAs. A few years after its demise, it became trendy to own a PDA despite the fact that the size and basic functionality of the Newton and the new generations of PDAs were the same. The impact and influence of trends and fads is heavily tied to culture because some cultures not only have consumers who desire and value one quality over another, but may also have more early adopters who are willing to try and embrace new technologies. In Singapore, for example, text messaging on a mobile phone has been one of the most prevalent fads since the early 1990s among the younger generation, despite the apparent clumsiness and slow character entry using the phone's numeric keypad—a nightmare that will make any usability engineer cringe.

Summary

Perception should never be assumed to be accurate and true to the actual duration. Whereas actual duration reflects objective time, perceived duration reflects subjective psychological time, which is susceptible to varying degrees of distortion. In addition to differentiating between actual and perceived durations, one has to consider user tolerance, which can be influenced by both temporal factors (such as benchmarks and standards) and nontemporal factors (such as bias and trends).

Rabbit Hole

Perception Management

Geelhoed, E., P. Toft, S. Roberts, and P. Hyland (1995). To influence time perception. *CHI'95 Mosaic of Creativity,* 272–273.

Hui, M. K. and D. K. Tse (1996). What to tell consumers in waits of different lengths: An integrative model of service evaluation. *Journal of Marketing,* 60, 81–90.

Katz, K., B. Larson, and R. Larson (1991). Prescriptions for the waiting in line blues entertain, enlighten and engage. *Sloan Management Review,* Winter, 44–53.

Kellaris, J. J. and R. J. Kent (1992). The influence of music on consumers' temporal perceptions: Does time fly when you're having fun? *Journal of Consumer Psychology,* 1, 365–376.

Leclerc, F. (2002). How should one be told to hold? *Advances in Consumer Research,* 28, 78.

North, A. C., D. J. Hargreaves, and J. McKendrick (1999). Music and on-hold waiting time. *British Journal of Psychology,* 90, 161–164.

Oakes, S. (2003). Musical tempo and waiting perceptions. *Psychology & Marketing,* 20, 685–705.

Sasser, W. E., M. Olsen, and D. D. Wychoff (1978). *The Management of Service Operations.* Boston: Allyn & Bacon. (Author's note: Installed mirrors near elevators reduce perceived waiting time!)

Perceived Time

Allan, L. G. (1979). The perception of time. *Perception & Psychophysics,* 26, 340–354.

Eisler, H. (1975). Subjective duration and psychophysics. *Psychological Review,* 82, 429–450.

Fraisse, P. (1984). Perception and estimation of time. *Annual Review of Psychology,* 35, 1–36.

Hicks, R. E., G. W. Miller, and M. Kinsbourne (1976). Prospective and retrospective judgments of time as a function of amount of information processed. *The American Journal of Psychology,* 89, 719–730.

Loehlin, J. C. (1959). The influence of different activities on the apparent length of time. *Psychological Monographs,* 73, 1–27.

Loftus, E. F. (1987). Time went by so slowly: Overestimation of event duration by males and females. *Applied Cognitive Psychology,* 1, 3–13.

Merikle, P. M. and S. Joordens (1997). Parallels between perception without attention and perception without awareness. *Consciousness and Cognition,* 6, 219–236.

Thomas, E. A. C. and W. B. Weaver (1975). Cognitive processing and time perception. *Perception & Psychophysics,* 17, 363–367.

Classic Experiments on Memory

Loftus, E. F. and J. C. Palmer (1974). Reconstruction of automobile destruction. *Journal of Verbal Learning and Verbal Behavior,* 13, 585–589.

Miller, G. A. (1956). The magical number seven, plus or minus two: Some limits on out capacity for processing information. *The Psychological Review,* 63, 81–97. (Author's notes: One the most seminal papers on memory. Reproduced with permission at www.musanim.com/miller1956/.)

User Tolerance

Dellaert, B. G. C. and B. E. Kahn (1999). How Tolerable Is Delay? Consumers' evaluations of internet websites after waiting. *Journal of Interactive Marketing,* 13, 41–54.

Goodin, R. E., J. M. Rice, M. Bittman, and P. Saunders (2005). The time-pressure illusion: Discretionary time vs. free time. *Social Indicators Research,* 73, 43–70.

Hancock, P. A. and J. L. Weaver (2005). On time distortion under stress. *Theoretical Issues in Ergonomics Science,* 6, 193–211.

Osuna, E. E. (1985). The psychological cost of waiting. *Journal of Mathematical Psychology,* 29, 82–105.

Pruyn, A. and A. Smidts (1999). Customers' reactions to waiting: Effects of the presence of 'fellow sufferers' in the waiting room. *Advances in Consumer Research,* 26, 211–216.

Saffo, P. (1996). The consumer spectrum. *In Bringing Design to Software,* T. Winograd (Ed.), 87–99. Reading, MA: Addison-Wesley (Author's note: Read the section "Threshold of Indignation.")

3

User and System Response Times

Well before personal computers became popular, researchers knew that the timing between the user's command and the system's response would be critical in maintaining an optimal user experience. In many ways, human-computer interaction is like a conversation. This chapter introduces both user and system response times and discusses various industry standards on maximum acceptable system response times.

The Silicon-Carbon Conversation

Dave wanted his computer to simply open the doors, but his computer is not obeying. "I'm sorry, Dave, I'm afraid I can't do that," the computer, named HAL, said matter-of-factly. Puzzled, Dave asked for an explanation, "What's the problem?" Sounding a little more sinister this time, HAL replied, "I think you know what the problem is just as well as I do."

That was a memorable scene from the 1968 movie *2001: A Space Odyssey*. Although we have yet to produce a computer that can function like HAL (and we probably don't want to), we are in constant communication with the computer. Sometimes we are feeding information to the computer, and other times the computer is providing information to us. Because information flows both ways in human-computer interaction, we have an interaction that is *conversational* in nature.

As in human-to-human conversations, there are etiquettes. Specifically, timing matters in a conversation between human and computer. For example, in human-to-human conversations, a pause to a simple question can have interesting interpretations and implications. Consider the following dialogue between Homer and Marge Simpson from an episode of the cult cartoon hit *The Simpsons*:

Homer: "Marge, do you respect my intelligence?"

(about four seconds later)

Marge: "Yes."

Homer: "Okay!… Wait a minute. Why did it take you so long to say yes?"

(about four seconds later)

Marge: "No reason."

Homer: "Okay!… Wait a minute. Were you humoring me?"

(about four seconds later)

Marge: "Yes."

Homer: "Okay!… Wait a minute. That's bad!"

The four-second pauses can be interpreted as hesitation because it should not have taken Marge that much time to respond to Homer's question. Likewise, when the computer takes several seconds to respond to a simple command, the user naturally feels that something is wrong with the computer.

Defining Response Time

Somewhere in a conference room in Silicon Valley, a decision needs to be made on how fast a particular feature of a solution should be. After much debate and bickering, someone in the room mentions learning something in a college psychology class about human reaction time of 200 milliseconds. This nugget of knowledge seems to put the debate to a satisfactory end, as seen by the approving nods across the room. Two hundred milliseconds it is. Case closed.

What's wrong with this scenario and the outcome? Short answer: There might be a confusion here with two very different timings. Unless the group is discussing a time-sensitive or mission-critical solution, how fast a particular feature should be typically has nothing to do with how fast users can react.

At the simplest level, response time can be defined as simply the start and end of a process or an interaction. The start of any process or interaction can be triggered automatically, such as a scheduled notification, or triggered in response to a command, such as the user pressing a key. In either case, this essentially starts the stopwatch, so to speak. Typically, the response itself is an observable action or result that stops the stopwatch, marking the tail end of the response time (see Figure 3.1). In some cases, it may be more accurate to define the completion of the result as the end of a process. For example, the initial loading of some text on a Web page hardly qualifies as marking the end of a Web page loading. In this case, the end of the process is when the page loads in full and is perceived ready and usable by the user.

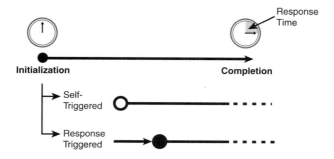

FIGURE 3.1

Response times can be triggered automatically or triggered in response to a command. In either case, the response time is marked by a start time and a completion time.

If the user is the one who starts or triggers a process (such as by pressing a key), the time between the user wanting to start the process to the moment the observable action is made is called the *user response time*. As mentioned, such initialization can either be self-triggered (such as powering up the computer in the morning) or triggered in response to an external factor (such as choosing among a list of results displayed on the screen). Determining an exact start time for self-triggered initialization is arbitrary because there are many unobservable mental processes—decision making, recognition, and so forth—that go into preparing for the actual observable gesture. In most cases, you will be dealing with the latter, where initialization results as a response to something the computer presented.

In the other direction, you have system-initiated processes. Again, this may be self-triggered (such as a scheduled notification to download updates) or, more commonly, triggered by the user (such as a mouse click to start an application). Between the initialization and the completion, the computer will take time to detect the user's input (mouse click) and then perform some function or exhibit some behavior (searching through the database), finally arriving at state where the process completes (returning the results). The time taken from one end to the other is most commonly called *system response time*. This is consistent to Shneiderman's definition: "The system's *response time* is the number of seconds that it takes from the moment a user initiates an activity (usually by pressing an Enter or Return key) until the computer begins to present results on the screen or printer."

The Conversation

For mainstream users, a typical interaction with the computer involves the combination of providing input to the computer (entering data, issuing commands, indicating choices, etc.) and receiving a sequence of responses from the computer (displaying results, animation, crunching data, etc.). This is illustrated in Figure 3.2. In all likelihood, these sequences are overlapping in that the users are already thinking and planning a few steps ahead while the computer is still responding to the first command.

Suppose you have to send an e-mail with your e-mail program. Chances are, before you read the first word of this sentence, your brain had already listed the correct steps to accomplish the task. Whereas a new user may use the careful step-by-step "cookbook recipe" approach of carefully performing a sequence of steps to get a task done (for example, when applying the red-eye reduction feature in a photo-editing program), a savvy user will more likely mentally lock into the final goal and work toward that goal using memorized steps. A majority of users will be in this latter group.

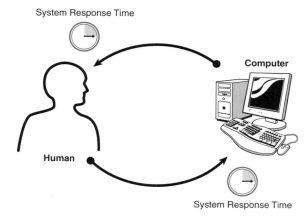

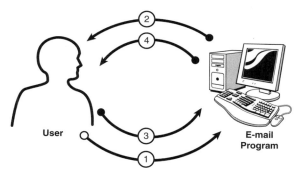

1. User wants to see new e-mails, so he double-clicks on icon on desktop.

2. System detects user's request and launches the e-mail program.

3. User sees that program is ready, so he clicks on a Check Mail button.

4. Program checks for new mail and informs the user that there is new mail.

FIGURE 3.2

Top: Human-computer interaction as a conversational process
Bottom: Example of how a typical interaction occurs

User Response Times

Back to the Silicon Valley debate. It does takes around 200 milliseconds for humans to give a simple response to the presentation of a simple stimulus. That is, suppose that someone is instructed to press a key as soon as a dot appears on a screen. The average elapsed time between the appearance of the dot and the key press will be around a fifth of a second. This timing is commonly known as *simple reaction time* and is typically measured in the lab with simple responses such as finger tapping.

Although more-complex responses involve more movements, which result in slower reaction time, some complex responses can be completed close to a fifth of a second with training. Champion fast-draw shooters, for instance, can draw their guns from the holster and fire a shot in about 200 milliseconds. For the rest of us, 200 milliseconds is about how fast we can make a simple observable action in response to the appearance of some stimulus (sound, object, etc.) in the outside world. This explains why it is advantageous for game show contestants to keep their hands on the buzzer rather than in their pockets!

If the task requires more thinking, such as making a response to a red dot but not a blue one, reaction time will slow down. The notion that *choice reaction time* increases as the number of choices increases was first studied in the 1800s, and it was later scientifically modeled as the Hick-Hyman Law, which is essentially a human performance model that views humans as information processors. Just as any other form of processor, the information processor has limitations. Simply put, when there is a lot of information to process, the processor will take more time. One way to simplify this concept is to compare filling a swimming pool with water using a garden hose or a fire hose. The former has a smaller bandwidth and will logically need more time to fill the pool. Hick's experiment shows that as the number of choices increases from two to ten,[1] reaction time increases from around 200 to 500 milliseconds.

Speed-Accuracy Tradeoff

One reason why understanding user response time is important is the *Speed-Accuracy Tradeoff*. When people try to perform a task as fast as possible, a lot of mistakes are made. Vice versa, when people try to make as few mistakes as possible, speed is compromised. This tradeoff has been well studied in psychology. In the 1952 study conducted by Hicks, for example, participants were encouraged to respond as fast as possible in one set of trials and then encouraged to respond as accurately as possible in another set of trials. In the first set of trials, participants were relatively faster, but performance was riddled with errors. In the latter, overall accuracy was higher, but response times were relatively slower.

Many factors lead to a decrease in human response time (getting faster in responding). Mere practice shortens user response time. This decrease in response time is typically viewed as a measure of performance improvement and typically described by the

---

[1] In Hick's study, information was quantified in bits. Users have to selectively respond to an increasing number of choices. A two-choice trial carries one bit because it is a binary decision that the user needs to make. A four-choice trial carries two bits, and so on.

Power Law of Practice, which essentially states people will start learning a novel task slowly, but they will gradually improve their timing in doing the task. That is, if you were to plot the timing performance on a graph, you should be able to see an initial learning curve, followed by a flattening that suggests that learning is stabilizing. Back to the Speed-Accuracy Tradeoff, you can probably say that the leveling point is a comfort zone where people feel that they are making efficient progress both in terms of speed and accuracy in performing a specific task. Figure 3.3 illustrates the Speed-Accuracy Tradeoff and the Power Law of Practice.

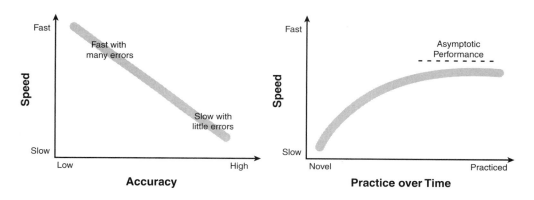

FIGURE 3.3

Left: Speed-Accuracy Tradeoff. When there is a focus on speed, accuracy will be compromised, and vice versa. Right: Power Law of Practice. Over time, the time taken to complete a new task gets shorter.

When users are forced by the user interface (UI) to accomplish some task by a certain time, errors will begin to surface. Apart from games (where imposing time constraints actually makes the game challenging) or time-critical applications (such as medical instruments or weapon systems), take care when imposing time limits on users, especially in situations where users have to make a decision. Conversely, when the software is designed to require accurate and precise information from the user, the user will be slowed down. For example, most graphical controls, such as buttons and scrollbars, have generous regions where users can click to invoke some command. Imagine if these controls were scaled down to just a few pixels. Under such a scenario, it should be evident why user response time would be affected. This simple phenomenon is captured in a well-known principle called *Fitts' Law*. Similarly, when the system asks the user to make a decision based on some ambiguous information, the user will be slowed down unnecessarily—an example of the *Hick-Hyman Law* (see Figure 3.4).

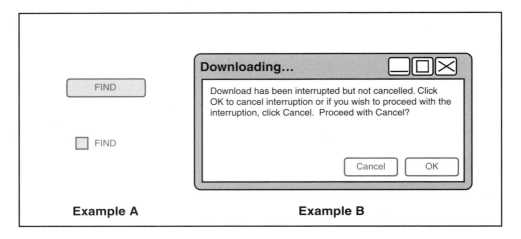

FIGURE 3.4

Left: An example of Fitts' Law. When the clickable area of the Find button is reduced, user response time will be relatively slower. Right: An example of Hick-Hyman Law. As the mental workload increases, user response time will be compromised, too.

System Response Time

Complementary to user response time is system response time. In the context of human-computer interaction, system response time must be defined from the user's perspective. As an example, suppose a user enters a search term in a search engine and clicks the Search button. As far as the user is concerned, clicking the button marks the start of the process, and the subsequently displayed results mark the completion of that process (see Figure 3.5). Back-end processes and other operations that comprise the search are meaningless to the average mainstream user. What is important is what the user experiences.

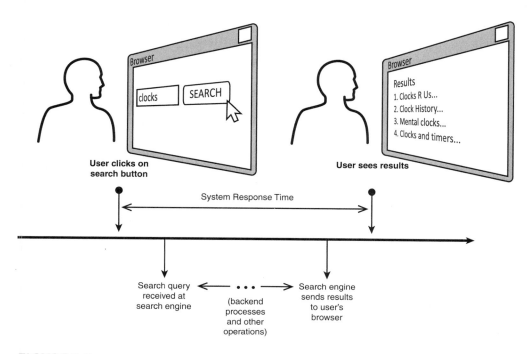

FIGURE 3.5

In the human-computer interaction context, system response time must be measured from the moment a user makes an observable action to the moment the user sees a result.

In defining and calculating system response times, you must factor in the time taken to provide the action and the time required for the user to detect a response from the computer. This applies not only to a relatively tangible duration, such as the one in Figure 3.5, but also to processes with very short durations. Consider the example illustrated in Figure 3.6. Research shows that keyboard delays can range from 11 milliseconds to 73 milliseconds, so there might be some overhead before a character is rendered. Depending on the refresh rate of the computer monitor, there might also be some latency before the character is painted on the screen. Therefore, relying entirely on the timing obtained in code may prove insufficient.

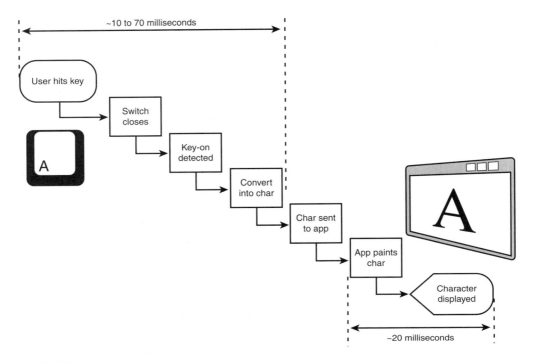

FIGURE 3.6

Research shows that keyboard latency can range anywhere between 10 and 70 milliseconds. Depending on the refresh rate of the computer monitor, there might also be some latency before the character is painted on the screen. What happens in between these two processes can typically be determined in code.

Industry Standards for System Response Times

System response time is largely driven by hardware. Increased processing power, for instance, can make the actual search operation faster, which reduces system response time. Tapping the power of hardware, software influences system response time, too. However, software by itself can demonstrate compelling timing improvements. Improved compression algorithms, as a simple example, even without souped-up hardware, can expedite the transmission of data, which also reduces system response time. Another related but less-conspicuous factor that affects system response time is design. That is, even with the latest software technology riding on the most powerful hardware under the hood, if the system is ill-designed with functionless redundancies and unnecessary overheads, system response time can still be compromised.

Despite the fact that system response time is driven by hardware, influenced by software, and optimized by design, system response time in a human-computer interaction context must take into account physiological and psychological constraints. For example, we know that most English readers cannot read more than four or five words a second—a reflection of both physiological and psychological limitations—so there is little value in presenting a stream of textual information that is too rapid to read or a block of text with insufficient time to read, let alone comprehend. In light of this, several industry standards of system response time have been developed to guide UI design.

MILLER (1968)

In a 1968 paper titled "Response Time in Man-Computer Conversational Transactions," R. B. Miller described several scenarios of human-computer interactions representing an "exhaustive listing and definition of different classes of human action and purpose at terminals of various kinds." This is one of the earliest, if not the earliest, guidelines on system response time. The language that Miller used in the scenarios, such as "System, can you do work for me?" ought not to be taken literally, but was fully intended by Miller to "simplify communication to the reader of the report." Table 3.1 displays a subset of the scenarios depicted by Miller.

Table 3.1 Subset of Guidelines in Miller (1968)

Topic	Timing (sec)
Response to control activation	0.1 to 0.2
Response to "System, are you listening?"	3
Response to "System, can you do work for me?"	2 (simple) 5 (complex)
Response to "System, do you understand me?"	2 to 4
Response to identification	0.4 to 0.5 (feedback) 0.2 (confirmation)
Response to "Here I am; what work should I do next?"	10 to 15
Response to a simple inquiry of listed information	2
Response to a simple inquiry of status	7 to 10
Response to a complex inquiry in tabular form	4
Response to a request for the next page	1
Response to "Now, run my problem."	15

Table 3.1 Subset of Guidelines in Miller (1968) (continued)

Topic	Timing (sec)
Response to the delay following a keyboard entry versus a light-pen entry of category for inquiry	3 (keyboard) 2 (light pen)
Graphic response from light pen	0.1
Response to complex inquiry in graphic form	2 to 10

MIL-STD 1472

A Department of Defense effort, the MIL-STD 1472F, also known as the *Department of Defense Design Criteria Standard: Human Engineering* (revision F) , is a 219-page document that details guidelines from fine to coarse settings for knobs to the color coding of simple indicator lights. The official purpose of the document is to "present human engineering design criteria, principles, and practices to achieve mission success through the integration of the human into the system, subsystem, equipment, and facility, and achieve effectiveness, simplicity, efficiency, reliability, and safety of system operation, training, and maintenance." Timing-specific metrics are conveniently summarized for the reader in Table XXII in the document, a subset of which are listed here in Table 3.2.

Table 3.2 Subset of Guidelines in MLT-STD 1472

Action	Definition	Timing (sec)
Key response	Key depression until positive response (e.g., click)	0.1
Key print	Key depression until the appearance of a character	0.2
Page turn	End of request until the first few lines are visible	1.0
Page scan	End of request until the text begins to scroll	0.5
XY entry	From selection of field until visual verification	0.2
Function	From selection of command until response	2.0
Pointing	From input of point to display point	0.2
Sketching	From input of point to display of line	0.2
Local update	Change to image using local database (e.g., new menu list from the display buffer)	0.5
Host update	Change where data is at the host in readily accessible form (e.g., a scale change of an existing image)	2.0
File update	Image update requires an access to a host file	10.0

Action	Definition	Timing (sec)
Inquiry (simple)	From command until display of a commonly used message	2.0
Inquiry (complex)	Response message requires seldomly used calculations in graphic form	10.0
Error feedback	From entry of input until an error message appears	2.0

ESD/MITRE

These 1986 guidelines published by the MITRE Corporation were prepared for and sponsored by the U.S. Air Force. However, the authors clearly expected the guidelines to be applicable to and applied by teachers, students, human-factor practitioners, researchers, system analysts, and software designers. Formally designated as the ESD-TR-86-278, the *Guidelines for Designing User Interface Software* comprises 944 guidelines covering topics in data entry, data display, sequence control, user guidance, data transmission, and data protection. The guidelines borrow from other existing guidelines, including an earlier revision of the MLT-STD 1472. Table 3.3 summarizes some guidelines that pertain to system response times.

Table 3.3 Subset of Guidelines in ESD/MITRE

Section	Topic/Action	Timing (sec)	Guidance
1.0/4	Fast response	0.2	Maximum time for delays in displayed feedback for normal operation
1.1/5	Fast acknowledgment of entry	0.2	Maximum time to acknowledge the entry of a designated position
1.1/7	Responsive cursor control	0.5	Maximum time for moving the cursor from one position to another
2.7.1/6	Fast response to display request	0.5 to 1.0	System response to a simple request for data display
3.0/28	Appropriate computer response time	0.5 to 1.0 2.0	System response to a control entry System response to simple entries
3.0/19	Control availability	0.2	Maximum time for control delays or lockouts
4.3/11	Appropriate response time for error messages	2.0 to 4.0	Display error message

TAFIM

The *Technical Architecture Framework for Information Management* (TAFIM) is an eight-volume documentation also developed by the Department of Defense (DoD) in 1996 to "provide guidance for the evolution of the DoD technical infrastructure, defining the services, standards, design concepts, components, and configurations that can be used to guide the development of technical architectures that meet specific mission requirements." Specific guidelines on human-computer interface are found in the last volume, and timing-specific guidelines are shown in Table 3.4.

Table 3.4 Subset of Guidelines in TAFIM

Section	Topic/Action	Timing (sec)	Guidance
6.6.2	Work-in-progress window	5 sec	For simple requests that can be processed under this time, provide simple visual feedback via a brief message. If the request response exceeds this time, the application should provide a window to indicate work in progress.
8.3.1.14	Control	5 to 200 ms	System response time.
8.3.1.15	Feedback	15 sec	If the user waits more than this time, provide a periodic indication of normal operation.

Summary

Human-computer interaction is conversational in nature, and therefore timing in both user response time and system response time is critical. For user response time, it is important to remember that when users have to focus on speed, accuracy is compromised, and vice versa. For system response times, several industry standards are available that provide guidance on the maximum acceptable response time. Although these guidelines offer concrete metrics to work with, they are based on the performance of the hardware and software available at the time when the guidelines were published. Therefore, take care when following these guidelines. In the next chapter, we consider an alternate, user-centric approach to system response times.

Rabbit Hole

Human Response Times

Card, S. K., J. D. Mackinlay, and G. G. Robertson (1991). *The Information Visualizer: An Information Workspace.* ACM Conference on Human Factors in Computing Systems (CHI '91), 181–188.

Luce, R. D. (1986). *Response Times: Their role in inferring elementary mental organization.* New York: Oxford University Press.

Ulrich, R. and M. Giray (1989). Time resolution of clocks: Effects on reaction time measurement—Good news for bad clocks. *British Journal of Mathematical & Statistical Psychology, 42,* 1–12.

System Response Time

Beringer, J. (1992). Timing accuracy of mouse response registration on the IBM microcomputer family. *Behavior Research Methods, Instruments, & Computers, 24,* 486–490.

Miller, R. B. (1968). Response time in man-computer conversational transaction. Fall Joint Comp. Conf. U.S.A., 267–277.

Shimizu, H. (2002). Measuring keyboard response delays by comparing keyboard and joystick inputs. *Behavior Research Methods, Instruments, & Computers, 34,* 250–256.

Shneiderman, B. (1984). Response time and display rate in human performance with computers. *Computing Survey, 16,* 265–285.

Speed-Accuracy Tradeoff

Fitts, P. M. (1966). Cognitive aspects of information processing: III. Set for speed versus accuracy. *Journal of Experimental Psychology, 71,* 849–857.

Pachella, R. G. and R. W. Pew (1968). Speed-accuracy tradeoff in reaction time: Effect of discrete criterion time. *Journal of Experimental Psychology, 76,* 19–24.

Hick-Hyman Law and Fitts' Law

Fitts, P. M. (1954). The information capacity of the human motor system in controlling the amplitude of movement. *Journal of Experimental Psychology, 47,* 381–391.

Hick, W. E. (1952). On the rate of gain of information. *Quarterly Journal of Experimental Psychology, 4,* 11–26.

Hyman, R. (1953). Stimulus information as a determinant of reaction time. *Journal of Experimental Psychology,* 45, 188–196.

Seow, S. C. (2005). Information Theoretic Models of HCI: A comparison of Hick-Hyman Law and Fitts' Law. *Human-Computer Interaction,* 20, 315–352.

Industry Standards

Department of Defense Design Criteria Standard: Human Engineering. MIL-STD 1472F. (Author's note: Available online at http://hfetag.dtic.mil/docs-hfs/mil-std-1472f.pdf.)

Department of Defense Technical Architecture Framework for Information Management (TAFIM). Volume 8: DoD Human Computer Interface Style Guide.

Smith, S. L and J. N. Mosier (1986). *Guidelines for Designing User Interface Software: ESD-TR-86-278.* Bedford, MA: The MITRE Corporation.

4

Responsiveness

Responsiveness is typically used to describe a characteristic of a solution, but if the solution is used by humans, it cannot be properly defined without the user. Whereas hardware and software will continually improve, human perceptual abilities will remain unchanged. This chapter introduces a way to classify responsiveness according to the general perception of what is instantaneous, immediate, continuous, and captive.

What Is Responsiveness?

The definition of *responsiveness* in the context of computing can sometimes be as elusive as the definition of beauty in poetry or style in fashion—you know it when you see it. You are going to need more formal metrics to design responsive computer systems. In the preceding chapter, human-computer interaction is related to human-human interaction because both are conversational in nature. If this analogy is accurate, it should be possible to define software responsiveness in the same way as human conversation responsiveness. Three important characteristics of responsiveness are that it is *relative* to the type of interaction in question, *subjective* in that users may have different levels of tolerance and interpretation of it, and *nonexclusive* in its form so that any indirect indication can also serve as a gauge of responsiveness.

Responsiveness Is Relative to the Interaction

Is five seconds too long for a response? Well, it really depends on what is being asked. Suppose you spot a familiar face at a party, decide to approach the individual, and ask, "John Sperling, right?" In all likelihood, a five-second delay before a response from the individual will be odd indeed. However, suppose the individual is caught off-guard by a stranger with an unexpected question (for example, "You handled the Mitsubishi account six years ago with Mike, right?"); a five-second delay before a response might not be that unreasonable because it would be normal to take some time to recollect.

The same applies in the human-computer interaction context. Different forms of interactions will have different windows of acceptable response times. For example, the time between pressing a key and having the character appear after the insertion point (the blinking vertical line) should be much shorter than when clicking a button to reach a website and having the browser load the Web page fully. Therefore, evaluating all forms of responsiveness against one scale (very fast to very slow) or setting a cut-off (< 20 milliseconds = fast) is not taking the *relative* nature of responsiveness into consideration.

A Delay Is Subjectively Perceived

Back to the familiar face at the party: Suppose you have asked the individual if he was someone you knew, but he has been remained silent for well over five seconds. What would take him so long to respond to you? Perhaps he has a hearing problem and didn't even hear the question. Maybe he heard your question but is trying in vain to remember who you are. It could also be possible that he is not John Sperling or does not even understand English. It may even be possible, especially considering the technological trends these days, that John Sperling is unable to respond because he is actually having a cell phone conversation using an inconspicuous Bluetooth headpiece.

Likewise in the human-computer interaction context, there may be many reasons why a system is not responding as promptly as it should. Consider the typical example of attempting to reach a website (see Figure 4.1). To begin with, the Internet connection might not be established at all. The URL entered might be incorrect. The website might be receiving a lot of traffic during that particular time. Perhaps the Internet service provider (ISP) has disconnected service for some reason. For typical users, especially those who might not be technologically savvy, the interpretation is generally limited to a few usual suspects, such as the website or the browser.

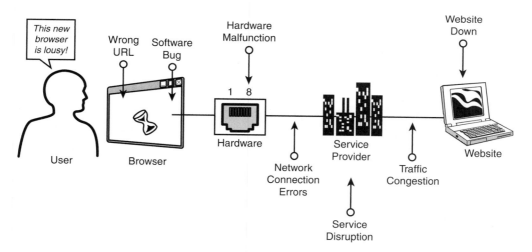

FIGURE 4.1

There might be several reasons why a particular Web page is not loading in a browser, but to the average user there will probably be just a few subjective interpretations of what is causing the failure.

Leaving users to guess why the system is not responding is the same as leaving a person to guess why a verbal response is not forthcoming in a conversation. When the user interface (UI) does not adequately communicate to the user its progress, users will likely want to quickly assign the blame to something. Occam's Razor—the simplest explanation is the best one—seems to hold true when it comes to pointing fingers: The newly installed browser is to blame for the slow connection, the management information system is poorly designed because it takes "forever" to display data from corporate, and so on. Thus, interpretations of delays are *subjective* because a user who is savvy might be more sympathetic and tolerant than another who is not.

Body Language Counts As a Response

Had it been true that John is having a cell phone conversation using a Bluetooth device, it would still be possible to give some indication to "postpone" his response through some nonverbal cues such as holding up a finger to give a "one-moment" signal. It is also normal to combine both verbal expressions and nonverbal cues when communicating. Sometimes it is as explicit as a shoulder shrug to indicate that we don't know the answer or narrowing the eyebrows to express that we are thinking. Other times, it is subtle and less voluntary, such as what psychologist P. Ekman calls "microexpression"—facial expressions that last around a quarter of a second.

In the human-computer interaction, explicit UI cues (progress bars and such) aren't the only type of response; any form of indication can be interpreted as a response. Consider how a computer powers up. At many points during the boot, the computer screen may go blank or remain unresponsive for several seconds. However, most users are not concerned about the supposed unresponsiveness because they can hear the hard disk drive thrashing or see an LED blinking. Thus, responsiveness is *nonexclusive* because the "body language" of the system or any artifact or symptom that results from the system performing a task can be interpreted by the user as a gauge of the level of responsiveness. Just as in human-human interaction, such indications can function to help or hurt the communication.

Responsiveness Based on User Expectancy

While computer technology continues to evolve, general perceptual abilities remain relatively stable. Therefore, an approach to generalizing responsiveness to different technologies and making it applicable over time is to establish *user-centric* as opposed to *technology-centric* metrics. In other words, the metrics ought to be established based on what we know about users, not technology.

The most popular user-centric response time guidance comes from the work of S. Card and his colleagues at Palo Alto Research Center, Inc. (PARC). Popularized by J. Nielsen, the basic notion is that there are three important *time constants* in human-computer interaction. The first, termed the *perceptual processing time constant* at 0.1 second, in Nielsen's words, concerns "having the users feel that the system is reacting instantaneously." The second, the *immediate response time constant* at one second, sets the "limit for the user's flow of thoughts to stay uninterrupted." The last, *unit task time constant* at ten seconds, relates to the user's attention on any single particular task.

The work of Card and his colleagues represents an alternative way to look at responsiveness. In the following sections, we look at a similar user-centric framework based on what users expect. That is, instead of tying specific interaction to a metric (such as *Key Response: 0.1 second*), a range of time values (based on what is already known and empirically established) is used for each expectancy (*Instantaneity: 0.1 to 0.2 second*) to set a range of maximum acceptable response times. Specific interactions are then assigned with what users expect (such as *Key Response: Instantaneous*). In doing so, the framework can accommodate the new forms of interaction as they become available. Figure 4.2 illustrates this approach.

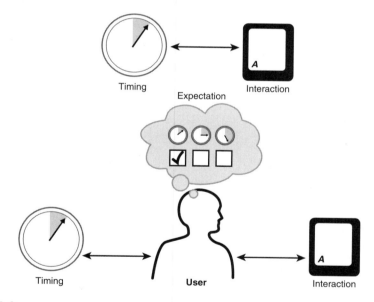

FIGURE 4.2

The model at the top of the diagram associates an interaction directly to a metric. The model at the bottom associates an interaction to what user expects (instantaneous, immediate, etc.). What the user expects is associated with the metric.

Instantaneous: 0.1 to 0.2 Second

When you flick a light switch, you expect the lights to turn on or off. In addition to the material and mechanical parts that constitute the switch, the laws of physics govern the instantaneous behavior and other properties of the switch. A graphical button in a software application, on the other hand, is not subject to the same physical laws (such as force, gravity, etc.) as the ones that govern the behavior of the light switch. For example, with a few lines of code, one can make the graphical button depress three seconds after it has been clicked by the user or even depress without user intervention. These behaviors are atypical for real physical buttons or switches because the "laws" that govern the behavior, as well as the look and feel of the graphical button, are artificially and arbitrarily determined in code. Figure 4.3 illustrates this analogy.

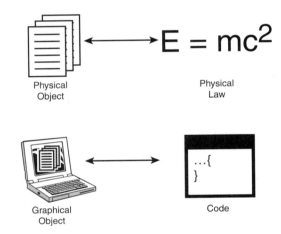

Physical Object   Physical Law

Graphical Object   Code

FIGURE 4.3

Physical objects observe physical laws, whereas objects generated by the computer observe whatever law is determined by programmatic code.

An obvious factor that adds to the desirability and usability of software is how well aspects of the software mimic objects and behaviors in the physical world. For example, it is common to assign a clicking sound and render visual effects, such as shading and shadow, to the buttons to make them sound and appear realistic. Another important "mimicry" is the responsiveness of the button. In most cases, all graphical controls or user input ought to have instantaneous behavior. More generally, all other forms of interaction that mimic some object in the physical world that has instantaneous behavior ought to show instantaneous responsiveness. This includes, but is not limited to, most forms of user input and their basic actions. For these interactions, the maximum response time—from an observable user-initiated action to an observable response by the computer—for simple input (such as key presses) must be less than 0.1 second and for more complex action, such as menu drop down, less than 0.2 second.

Immediate: 0.5 to One Second

Whereas we previously discussed instantaneous responsiveness, this next responsiveness class concerns immediate and prompt acknowledgment of information or instructions received and reflexive response to that information. This is the same as the beginning of a human-to-human conversation when one party initiates a face-to-face conversation by getting the attention of the other party by calling out his or her name:

> **John:** "Mary?"
>
> (less than one second later)
>
> **Mary:** "Yes, John."

If you substitute "one second" with "three seconds," it will become apparent that something is amiss in the conversation. As we discussed before, it is reasonable to interpret the delayed response as hesitance, inattentiveness, or even guilt. Similarly, replace the delay with "0.2 second," and you will begin to detect something aberrant about the conversation, too. In this latter case, you can interpret the fast response as anxiety, hyperactivity, or obsequiousness. Most people are subconsciously mindful of awkward pauses in conversations and subconsciously seek to fill the pauses. Card and his colleagues wrote the following:

> If it is more than a second, then either the listening party makes a backchannel response to indicate that he is listening (e.g. "uh-huh") or speaking party makes a response (e.g. "uh…") to indicate he is still thinking of the next speech.

In the context of human-computer interaction, the immediate responsiveness class sets the standard for acknowledging to the user that the user's information or instructions have been received, and if the request, instruction, or command is simple, the delivery of a full response. For example, if the user requests information that is perceived to be ready (such as some text on a Web page that falls outside of the viewable space on a browser), the expectation is that what is requested is already there and getting to it is merely navigating or panning it into view (see Figure 4.4). In such instances, the maximum limit of response time—again, from an observable user-initiated action to an observable response by the computer—is 0.5 to one second.

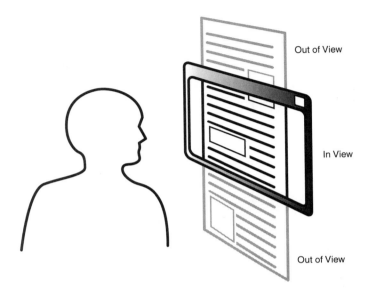

FIGURE 4.4

As far as the user is concerned, the application is showing what is in view, and other parts of the document are out of view. Therefore, navigating to another page is merely panning down or up the document, which should be immediate.

Continuous: Two to Five Seconds

Flow is a highly desirable quality in any conversation. In a typical human-to-human conversation, timing of information exchange between two parties is never constant (unless the two parties are rehearsing the lines from a script), in that the durations of pauses in speech vary. These variable pauses are normal and reflect time taken by each party to think and plan a response. When a response is too fast, it is not unreasonable to suspect that the response was prepared or not adequately contemplated. At the other extreme, when a response is punctuated by long awkward pauses, conversational flow can also be compromised. R. Miller wrote this:

> If you address another human being, you expect some communicative response within *x* seconds—perhaps two to four seconds.... In conversation of any kind between humans, silences of more than four seconds become embarrassing because they imply a breaking of the thread of communication.

To a certain degree, users understand that the computer needs time to "think." However, to maintain *continuity,* the system has to make *some* kind of response within a window of time. Miller makes an explicit recommendation: "The user will certainly have a continuity of ideas in mind when he makes complex inquiries. This particular inquiry should get a complete response within four seconds."

Two important things to keep in mind:

- First, this requirement to maintain continuity in a human-computer interaction is typically not imposed on the user. That is, the user doesn't need to respond to the computer within two to five seconds.

- Second, maintaining continuity can include instances when the system reports that it is unable to proceed or process the user's request. Sometimes the system cannot proceed because the user provided erroneous input, such as a typographical or syntactical error. In such cases where errors are *perceived* to be simple, the system ought to respond with an error message in well under two seconds. In cases where the system does accept the user's request but is unable to fulfill the request for a variety of reasons, the system ought to respond with an error message in no more than five seconds. Similarly, for any command or activity that is *perceived* to be simple by the user, the system ought to respond in close to two seconds. For those that are *perceived* complex, the system ought to respond in no more than five seconds. Figure 4.5 illustrates different degrees of hypothetical errors and a reasonable corresponding response time for each.

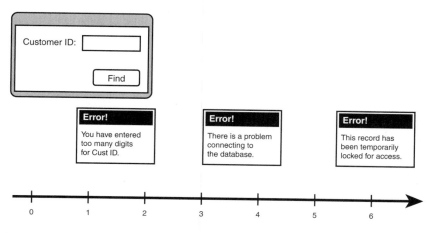

FIGURE 4.5

A hypothetical example of the timing associated with the levels of error. Simple errors, such as an incorrect input string, ought to be "caught" and responded to very early. More complex errors, such as the one shown on the far right, will reasonably take more time.

The lower and higher ends of the continuous responsiveness class also serve as good markers for the level of feedback to give while users await the completion of a process or activity. Under two seconds, no progress feedback is necessary because a delay of response under two seconds is typically tolerable (unless users expect instantaneous or immediate behavior). Beyond two seconds, however, one might want to consider simple progress feedback. Beyond five seconds, progress feedback is absolutely necessary. That is, periodic feedback of work in progress ought to be provided periodically between two and five seconds to assure the user that the system is not hung. You'll read more about this in Chapter 6, "Progress Indication."

Captive: Seven to Ten Seconds

Research has shown that people tend to abandon unresponsive websites after about eight to ten seconds. This range covers what MIT's T. Selker calls the "goldfish attention span" of nine seconds and Card and his colleagues' call the "unit task time constant" of ten seconds. The numbers from these and other studies point to user attention as a span of time roughly between seven and ten seconds, under and during which the solution has to do what it needs to do to keep the user's attention. Beyond this time, users tend to wander off or attend to other tasks. Obviously, some processes need more than ten seconds. Even with periodic feedback, patience to wait for a system response beyond more than ten seconds begins to wear thin. If the overall response time is more than 15 seconds, Miller advised in 1968:

> If he is a busy man, captivity of more than 15 seconds, even for information essential to him, may be more than an annoyance and disruption. It can readily become a demoralizer.... If, therefore, response delays of more than 15 seconds will occur, the system had better be designed to free the user from physical and mental captivity, so that he can turn to other activities and get his displayed answer when it is *convenient for him* to do so.

The rule of thumb is to deliver to the user useful or consumable information about an ongoing process every ten seconds or so. This practice is seen in many video streaming applications, where the application starts by storing a certain amount of buffer, and then begins playback of the buffered video while the remaining parts of the video are still being downloaded (see Figure 4.6). If it is not possible to deliver anything meaningful to the user in less than ten seconds, consider Miller's advice to make it possible to allow users to attend to other tasks.

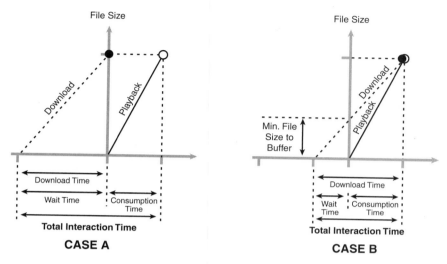

FIGURE 4.6

Two experiences in viewing video: In Case A, the user downloads the entire video before the playback starts. The total time taken for this interaction is the sum of the download time and the playback time. In Case B, playback starts as soon as a certain amount of buffer is available. Although the download time remains the same, since it overlaps with the consumption time, the total time taken for this interaction is shorter.

An important note to keep in mind is that the values represent the lower and upper limits for *maximum acceptable* response times. For example, a simple action, such as a key press, must complete at or below the lower end of the instantaneous class of 0.1 second. There is, however, a danger in making something too fast, which is explained in the next section. Figure 4.7 summarizes the four levels of responsiveness.

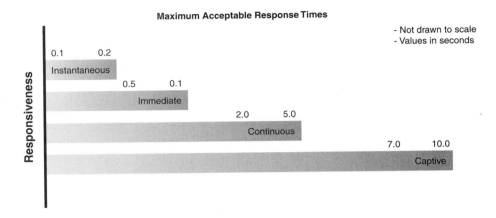

FIGURE 4.7

The maximum response times expressed as ranges for four classes of responsiveness.

Too Fast?

Can response times be too fast? Intuitively, it seems that as far as computing is concerned, the *faster* the *better*. After all, that has been the clear trend since the advent of modern computers. As previously argued, computing technology continues to evolve and improve, but the cognitive and perceptual abilities of the average human have remained relatively the same. This "mismatch" will cause usability problems when the computer is too fast for the user or when the user is too fast for the computer.

Computer Too Fast

It is not immediately intuitive, but it is possible for a solution or system to be *too fast* for users. This doesn't necessarily involve a slow user on a blazing computer because what is "too fast" is a relative concept. The computer may be responding with reasonable speed, but the user, for a variety of reasons, is having difficulty catching up. This is typical with users who are not dexterous with the input devices, users who require more time to plan their response because they are unfamiliar with the UI, or they need more decision-making or other cognitive-processing time.

Case in point: double-clicking behaviors in the Microsoft operating system environment. Suppose a user double-clicks the icon located on the desktop. Depending on the speed of the clicks (the time between press and release of the first and second clicks), different behaviors are triggered. In the Windows environment, by default, double-clicking must be performed within 500 milliseconds to launch an application or open a document. However, if the two clicks are made more than 500 milliseconds apart, the text label of the icon will go into active edit mode, where the name of the icon can be renamed. So instead of opening an application, users end up renaming the icon.

Studies show that age has a significant effect on how fast people can tap a single finger repetitively. The average fastest finger-tapping speed is around about 200 milliseconds for most adults. Not surprisingly, finger-tapping speed is expected to decline with age. Therefore, if the double-clicking speed is set too fast, certain users will not be able to accomplish the simple task of launching an application via double-clicking. Thankfully, Windows makes it possible to set that double-click speed.

Simply reducing the computer response time to match human response time is not an effective answer because it is generally favorable, in terms of performance, for a system to respond promptly to user interaction. The better solution is to minimally adjust the responsiveness of the computer so the users are able to have a certain degree of comfort as they are making the right progress, and the system is responding to their progress.

Deliberately slowing the system or your solution doesn't seem like a sound practice, but in some instances that is necessary. An excellent example where system response time is slightly compromised to provide the right experience for the user is the animated transition of windows. You can make minimizing and maximizing windows a little faster by removing the animation that shows the rapid shrinking and growing of the window and replacing it with an instantaneous toggling behavior between the various states. However, if you do so, users, particularly newer ones, might not fully understand how the windows are being handled. R. Rao expresses this same maxim: "Animating the transitions between one arrangement of the information and another allows the user to connect the before and the after. In well-designed transitions, the user will not wonder what is going on." Although these subtle UI visualizations don't add any functionality, the low-cost implementation makes the solution more usable. Figure 4.8 illustrates the minimizing of a window with and without animating transition.

As a relevant footnote, it is possible to exploit what is known as the *phi phenomenon* (also known as the illusory motion or apparent motion) to create the illusion of movement. First reported by psychologist M. Wertheimer, the phi phenomenon describes the visual illusion of movement of one object when two stationary instances of the object in different positions are rapidly presented in succession. Studies have pointed to 40 milliseconds (from the time the first instance disappears to the time the second instance appears) as an optimal duration for the illusion to take effect for short distances.

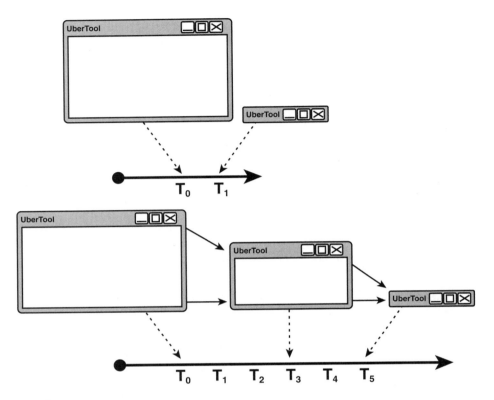

FIGURE 4.8

Top: When a window minimizes instantly without any visual effects to the user, especially new ones, it appears as if it vanished. Bottom: When a little bit more time is taken to animate the shrinking of the window into a minimized state, users get a better mental grasp of what was done to the window and where it has gone.

User Too Fast

The other scenario where the mismatch between human response time and system response time causes usability problems is when the user goes too fast for the computer. B. Shneiderman wrote, "There is also a danger in working too quickly. As users pick up the pace of a rapid interaction sequence, they may learn less, read with slower comprehension, make ill-considered decisions, and commit more data entry errors." The pitfalls Shneiderman refers to can be explained by the Speed-Accuracy Tradeoff mentioned in Chapter 3, "User and System Response Times."

Building "speed bumps" just to slow down users takes a toll on usability because it is natural for users to pick up some speed as they continue to engage in a particular task. As mentioned, timing performance for a new task improves over time and with practice (Power Law of Practice). By and large, this is a healthy and natural phenomenon because it is evidence that users are learning and getting better. However, as users reach this "terminal velocity," the risk of making errors increases. An example is when Windows users select multiple files, press the Delete key, and then follow that with the Enter key almost immediately to confirm their deletion. Because the operating system is not "fast enough" for the user, this leads to opening all selected files instead of confirming the deletion of all selected files.

Whereas some errors are minor, others can be detrimental. In either case, it can take a toll on users' productivity and usability if work has to be constantly corrected or redone. To handle this inevitable vulnerability, a common approach is to implement strategic "stop signs" that essentially ask users to verify their actions, especially when the action is critical, such as deleting a file, formatting a disk drive, or transmitting sensitive information. This ought to be implemented minimally. Another common practice is to incorporate capabilities that essentially allow users to step back in time to recover from a wrong course of action. Temporary deletion and undo features are great examples of this.

Summary

In modeling human-computer interaction after human-human interaction, we define responsiveness for the former as we do for the latter. The maximum acceptable time taken to prepare a response depends on the nature of the response; thus, responsiveness is *relative* to the type of interaction. Although many reasons may lead to longer-than-normal delays, there will likely be only a few *subjective* interpretations of what is happening. Lastly, responsiveness is *nonexclusive* in that any form of indication can function as an indication of responsiveness. In consideration of these factors, a user-centric responsiveness framework—based on the general perception of what is instantaneous, immediate, continuous, and captive—has been introduced.

Rabbit Hole

Microexpressions

Ekman, P. (2003). *Emotions Revealed: Recognizing faces and feelings to improve communication and emotional life.* New York: Times Books.

User-Centric Responsiveness

Card, S. K., J. D. Mackinlay, and G. G. Robertson (1991). *The Information Visualizer: An Information Workspace.* ACM Conference on Human Factors in Computing Systems (CHI '91), 181–188.

Dix, A. J. (1987). The myth of the infinitely fast machine. *People and Computers III – Proceedings of HCI'87,* D. Diaper and R. Winder (Eds.). Cambridge University Press. 215–228.

Geist, R., R. Allen, and R. Nowaczyk (1987). Towards a model of user perception of computer system response time. CHI + GI 1987, 249–253.

Miller, R. B. (1968). Response time in man-computer conversational transaction. Fall Joint Computer Conference U.S.A., 267–277.

Shneiderman, B. (1984). Response time and display rate in human performance with computers. *Computing Survey,* 16, 265–285.

User Flow

Csikszentmihalyi, M. (1990). *Flow: The Psychology of Optimal Experience.* New York: Harper and Row.

Ghanij, A. and S. P. Deshpandes (1994). Task characteristics and the experience of optimal flow in human-computer interaction. *Journal of Psychology,* 128, 381–391.

Rao, R. (1999). See and Go Manifesto. *Interactions,* September-October 1999. (Author's note: Available online at www.inxight.com/news/papers.html.)

Attention Span

Christakis, D. A., F. J. Zimmerman, D. L. DiGiuseppe, and C. A. McCarty (2004). Early television exposure and subsequent attentional problems in children. *Pediatrics,* 113, 708–713.

Turning into digital goldfish. http://news.bbc.co.uk/2/hi/science/nature/1834682.stm.

Web 'turns people into goldfish.' *The Inquirer.* February 22, 2002.

Zimmerman, F. J. and D. A. Christakis (2007). Associations between content types of early media exposure and subsequent attentional problems. *Pediatrics,* 120, 986–992.

5

Detecting Timing Differences

Understanding the ability to detect timing differences is critical to improving many aspects of human-computer interaction. Beneath a particular threshold, for example, differences become too small for human detection. Investing time, effort, and resources to deliver a difference that may not be noticeable might not be worthwhile. This chapter introduces basic concepts in human detection of timing changes to help define performance objectives, such as setting performance goals and determining regression allowance.

Telling the Difference

You are writing the specification for the next version of your CD-burning software. A particular feature of the current version of the software is taking 20 seconds to complete. The very talented developer on your team can bring the 20 seconds down to about 17 seconds, but it will take him two weeks to write the code. Figuring that three seconds is substantial, you decide that this improvement is worth the time and effort, so you officially add the improvement into the specification. What risks have you overlooked? Read on.

Having the innate ability to detect subtle differences is as practical in using computers as it is in performing day-to-day tasks because many measurements in life are done not with objective physical instruments but with subjective mental approximation. For instance, a seasoned chef will not need measuring utensils when putting together a signature dish. More likely, the chef can estimate how much of each ingredient to use because preparing the dish is a highly practiced task. That is, without using a measuring spoon or cup, the chef knows when there is too little or too much salt. The amount of salt the chef uses is different each time, and the acceptable quantity is really better represented as a range (see Figure 5.1). Somewhere beyond or beneath this range is when the chef will begin to detect that there is too little or too much.

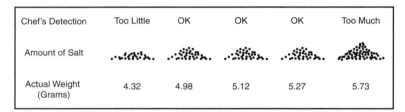

Chef's Detection	Too Little	OK	OK	OK	Too Much
Amount of Salt					
Actual Weight (Grams)	4.32	4.98	5.12	5.27	5.73

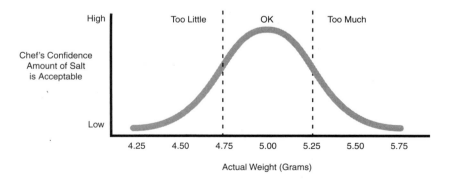

FIGURE 5.1

How much salt to use will not be exact but more likely be better represented as a range.

In the context of human-computer interaction, understanding the user's ability to detect timing differences is important in several contexts. In defining performance objectives, such as the fictitious scenario described at the beginning of the chapter, you need to consider whether a particular enhancement in performance is even detectable to your user. If the improvement is not even detectable, the return over investment will be questionable. Likewise, in the other direction, understand the window in which timing variations are not detectable, it is possible to determine how much performance degradation is acceptable, or what is referred to here as *regression allowance*.

D Levels

Chapter 4, "Responsiveness," introduced how to categorize various forms of interaction under classes of responsiveness depending on what the users expect. For example, most user interfaces (UIs) such as graphical buttons and other forms of interaction that mimic real-world physical objects must be designed to reflect instantaneous behavior. From another perspective, the process of determining the appropriate timing for a particular interaction can be viewed as a *D0* (zero-duration) scenario, in which you are just determining an appropriate timing independent of other timing measures, baselines, and other metrics.

There are instances when you are not dealing with a D0 scenario because there is a need to modify an existing duration. An example is when you have to determine whether a prospective improvement in timing is worth the investment. In the situation described at the beginning of this chapter, the proposed modification in design results is a three-second improvement for a process that typically takes 20 seconds. In such a scenario, you must determine the return on investment for reducing the 20 seconds down to 17 seconds. Because this deals with the modification of a single duration, these are classified as *D1* (single-duration) scenarios.

When two coexisting durations are involved, especially in competitive situations, one duration is inevitably compared to the other. For example, a search feature in an application is returning results in three seconds, and your current equivalent feature is doing the same in six seconds. It would be good to deliver, if possible, a response time shorter than three seconds, but sometimes it is acceptable to at least raise the bar (or in this example, lower the timing) just enough to, in G. Moore's lingo, *neutralize* the competition to eliminate *differentiation*. Moore's thinking is explained later, but for now, situations in which one duration is pitched against another is classified as *D2* (dual-durations) scenarios because an objective has to be set in consideration of two established durations. Figure 5.2 illustrates these three D levels.

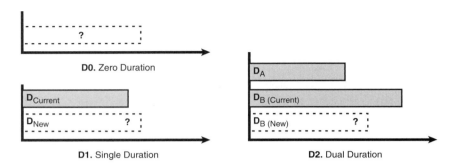

DO. Zero Duration

D1. Single Duration

D2. Dual Duration

FIGURE 5.2

An illustration of the three D levels. In the upper left, a duration is considered independently of other durations in a D0 scenario. In the lower left, a current duration ($D_{CURRENT}$) is to be modified (D_{NEW}) in a D1 scenario. In the last scenario, a new duration ($D_{B(NEW)}$) is to be determined for a current duration($D_{B(CURRENT)}$) in consideration of another duration (D_A).

The guidance for D0 scenarios is elaborated in Chapter 4. For the other two scenarios beyond D0, the objective is to understand the detection and perception of timing differences and how that applies to optimizing human-computer interactions. Two psychophysical principles—Weber's Law and Geometric Mean Bisection—relate well to D1 and D2 scenarios. The first principle concerns the detection of the difference in the magnitude of some property. In the computing context, this is applicable to comparing objective and relatively fixed durations, such as the response times of an application before and after some implementation. The second also concerns two magnitudes, but it focuses on determining a cutoff in light of two existing durations.

D1: Weber's Law

Imagine holding two weights in each hand: 1 pound in one hand and 2 pounds in the other. In all likelihood, you are able to determine which is heavier by merely holding the weights. Imagine repeating the same exercise with another pair of weights. This time, one weighs 21 pounds, and the other is a pound heavier at 22 pounds (see Figure 5.3). Despite the fact that both pairs differ by a pound, chances are you are not as reliable in telling which is heavier in the second exercise. Don't worry; your muscles in both arms are working just fine.

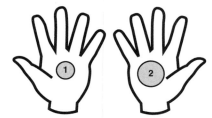

Comparison A. Easy discrimination of one-pound difference.

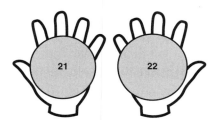

Comparison B. Difficult discrimination of one-pound difference.

FIGURE 5.3

It is fairly easy to tell the difference between 1 and 2 pounds in Comparison A (top). However, despite the same 1-pound difference in Comparison B, it is harder to tell the difference between 21 and 22 pounds.

This phenomenon was first observed by E. H. Weber, a German physician and a pioneer in experimental psychology. Working with G. T. Fechner, Weber formulated *Weber's Law*, which later evolved into the *Weber-Fechner Law*. Weber's Law premises on a key concept called *Just Noticeable Difference,* typically abbreviated in lowercase as jnd. Just as the name suggests, jnd is the minimum increase or decrease in magnitude of a property of a stimulus (the brightness of a light bulb, the volume of a static buzz, etc.) that is detectable or, as the name implies, noticeable. In the weight comparison example, you can determine your jnd by increasing the weight of the second weight until you begin to notice a difference.[1] Of course, as mentioned in the 1 versus 2 pounds and 21 versus 22 pounds examples, the jnd is different in each comparison. That is, you would probably need more than a 1-pound difference to start to tell which is heavier in the second

---

[1] Formally, being able to detect the difference 50% of the time would qualify the difference as the jnd. For example, if we run ten trials, and in six trials, the participants were able to detect the difference when the third pound was added, then the jnd is 3 pounds.

exercise. What Weber discovered was that the jnd increases as the magnitudes to be compared increases.[2]

In the context of time perception, Weber's Law is applicable whenever two durations are compared. Timing researchers typically divide the standard deviation by the mean to get what is called the *Weber fraction* or the *Weber ratio* (see Figure 5.4).

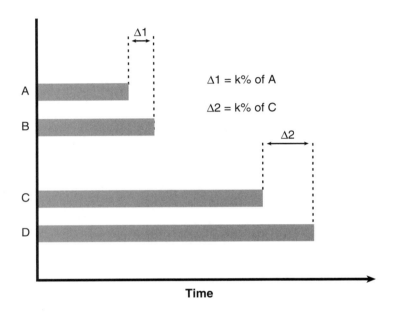

FIGURE 5.4

Suppose duration B is found to have the smallest possible difference from duration A in order for both durations to be distinguished, and likewise for durations C and D. Weber's Law states that the deltas (Δ1 and Δ2) in both comparisons are a constant ratio or percentage (k) of the shorter duration of each pair.

In layman's terms, the ability to detect the subtlest difference between any two durations, according to the theory, is a constant ratio (for example, between 10 and 12, between 20 and 24, or between 3000 and 3600). This ratio can be calculated by using the average and standard deviation of the data from an experimental task where participants are required to detect the difference between many pairs of duration. Studies

---

[2] Technically, according to the theory, jnd increases as a linear function of the *log* of the stimulus.

show that the Weber ratio for temporal discrimination (distinguishing between two durations) ranges from 7% to 18% for durations up to 30 seconds.

The 20% Rule

There are direct applications of Weber's Law and jnd concepts to human-computer inter-action. Based on data from human timing research, a good rule of thumb is to use a Weber ratio of 20% of the duration in question. You can either aim to stay beneath or exceed the cutoff depending on the context (see Figure 5.5). The following sections discuss two primary applications of the *20% Rule,* the first relating to staying beneath 20% and the second relating to exceeding the cutoff.

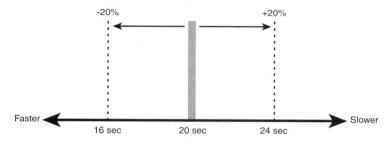

FIGURE 5.5

The 20% Rule suggests a lower limit and an upper limit of 20% of the duration in question (20 seconds in this figure) when considering improvement goals and regression allowance.

SETTING PERFORMANCE GOALS

There are many reasons why some existing duration needs to be shortened. Customers might be complaining about the sluggish performance of a particular search feature in your product. Perhaps usability tests are confirming that users are abandoning your website because the first page is loading too slowly. In these D1 scenarios, you have an existing duration that needs to be shortened to improve usability and satisfaction. The rule of thumb for such instances is to set an improvement in timing of at least 20% to ensure a perceptible improvement. For example, if the search feature is retrieving and returning results in ten seconds, it would be wise to deliver a new search response time of less than eight seconds.

Note that this is a general rule of thumb to increase the chance of mere detection. The Weber ratio just gives us an idea of how much delta ought to be attained to have a difference be *noticed* between two durations. A *noticeable* difference is not an adequate standard for a *meaningful* and *valuable* difference. Suppose a new compression technique reduces download speed from 30 seconds to 24 seconds—a reduction of 25%, which exceeds the prescribed 20%. Although users might notice the difference, they may not find it *meaningful* or impressive.

The rule merely provides a minimum standard of detection threshold. To attain a difference that is meaningful and valuable to your user, you definitely need to go well beyond a mere detection threshold. This doesn't mean that you should make everything as fast as possible every time. As mentioned in Chapter 4, it is possible for your system or your solution to be too fast. If a response time is already as fast as it can feasibly and technically be, and there are reasons to believe that customers or users are still dissatisfied, some tolerance management may be in order (see Chapter 10, "Techniques").

FINDING REGRESSION ALLOWANCE

In an ideal computing world, all the features in your product will get more compact, more elegant, more powerful, more secure, and more performant[3] with each version. In reality, tradeoffs are inevitable with each iteration. For example, an early version of your application might require 60MB of hard disk space for installation, but a later version might require ten times more space because of additional functionality. Conversely, an early version might start with 200 features and a sizable footprint,[4] but a later version has a substantially smaller footprint at the expense of a smaller set of features. Sometimes tradeoffs will involve a hit in timing performance. For instance, to include stronger security, your application might need to take additional time to load. This results in a performance degradation.

Because the 20% Rule relates to a prescribed cutoff where detection is possible, you can apply the rule in reverse to minimize the chance of detection in your favor. In this instance, you can use 20% as the upper limit of regression allowance. For example, if various implementations of the new security measure are yielding systematic performance degradation, you can use the rule as cutoff in deciding a balanced tradeoff (see Figure 5.6). Suppose that before implementation the application takes ten seconds to load. With the first implementation, an additional second is added to the load time. With the second implementation, an additional 1.5 seconds is added. With the third, three seconds is added. In this instance, the second implementation, which yields a 15% regression, is the best one without breaching the 20% cutoff.

---

[3] At the time of writing, this term *performant* is not included in a standard dictionary; however, it means "highly capable" or "effective" in French. The term is used frequently in the industry as an adjective to describe satisfactory performance.

[4] The amount of hard disk space or memory taken up by a software program or file.

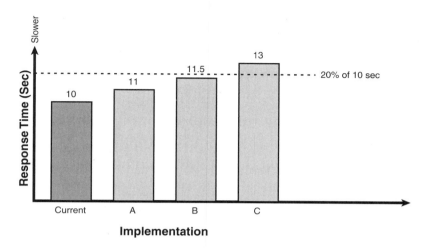

FIGURE 5.6

In this example, the current response time is at ten seconds, but incorporating a new feature is inevitably costing some overhead in timing performance. In this case, implementation B of the new feature is the best one because it doesn't breach 20% of the current response time, and thus reduces the chance of users detecting a difference.

D2: Geometric Mean Bisection

The push to deliver better timing performance doesn't always come from the need to deliver improvement because your customers or users are dissatisfied with the current performance. Often, you have to improve timing performance because a competitive equivalent of your product is delivering markedly better performance. Ideally, it makes sense to respond by outperforming the competition, but in reality, with a laundry list of constraints, that is not always possible.

When a product or service has differentiated itself from yours, it only makes sense to take appropriate steps to keep your product in the game. As mentioned, G. Moore highlights in his book *Dealing with Darwin* the benefits of neutralizing the differentiation:

> The first of the alternative desired outcomes is neutralization. Its goal is to eliminate differentiation by catching up either to a competitor's superior performance or to a market standard one has fallen short of.... Netscape achieved differentiation with the Internet browser; then Microsoft achieved neutralization. Citibank achieved differentiation with ATM machines in the 1970s; then all other banks achieved neutralization.

In other words, Moore is suggesting that sometimes, in lieu of outperforming the competition, it pays to make the minimal step of delivering performance that is on par with or at least close to the competition so that consumers begin to perceive neither one has a substantially higher value over the other (Figure 5.7).

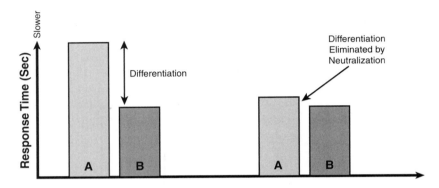

FIGURE 5.7

On the left, B has attained differentiation in delivering markedly better performance. On the right, A delivers performance close to that of B, thereby eliminating the differentiation by attaining neutralization.

The Not-by-Much Standard

The litmus test of Moore's differentiation elimination by neutralization is called the *not-by-much standard* because when placed side-by-side, detectable differences are present but not markedly so. For example, reviewers who are evaluating two or more products may conclude that one product is more superior than the other but *not by much*. When your product has attained the not-by-much standard, the differentiation created by the competition begins to diminish.

Suppose your company develops software for data backup and the current version of your product takes 60 seconds to back up 1GB of data. A competitor has delivered an equivalent product that takes only 30 seconds to do the same. Technical limitations and other constraints do not permit you to deliver sub-30-second performance but some improvement is technically feasible. How should you set the new performance objective? More specifically, what new timing should you aim for to begin to "neutralize the differentiation"? Where is the not-by-much standard cutoff? The cutoff in the hypothetical example, according to research in human timing, is at about 42 seconds. Where did this number come from?

Given two durations, one longer than the other, where is middle of the two? Many studies in animal timing, particularly conducted by R. Church of Brown University and his colleagues, show that the middle of two durations or the *bisection* is predictable but is not just the average of the two (see Figure 5.8). Fascinated by this robust finding in animals, such as rats and pigeons, other timing researchers tested bisection in human participants and found the same results: The midpoint between two durations was found not at the arithmetic mean (average) but at the geometric mean.

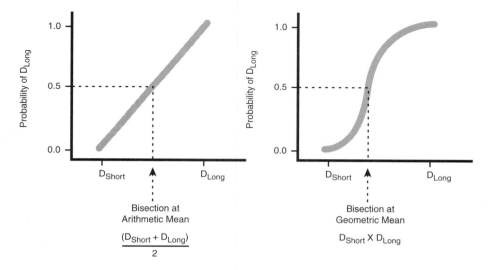

FIGURE 5.8

The left function shows that the middle of two durations is perceived to be at the arithmetic mean (average) of the two. Animal and human timing research has shown that this is not the case. The middle of two durations appears to be at the geometric mean, as shown on the right function.

DIFFUSING DIFFERENTIATION BY NEUTRALIZATION

The geometric mean for two values is simply the square root of the product of the values. In the preceding data backup example, given the two durations of 30 and 60 seconds, you can determine the geometric mean by finding the square root of the product of 30 and 60, which is 42. Research on bisection tells us that beyond the geometric mean, the probability of associating a value with the higher value of the two increases. That is, values above 42 will be perceived more like 60 than 30. Vice versa, values below 42 will be judged to be closer to 30 than 60. Therefore, the geometric mean marks the cutoff for the example in the next section, and setting a goal of under 42 seconds (the lower the better, of course) would theoretically secure the not-by-much standard.

MAINTAINING DIFFERENTIATION

Just as you can apply the 20% Rule to both determining improvement goals and regression allowance, you can apply the same not-by-much standard in the other direction. Suppose your product is leading the backup performance at 30 seconds per 1GB of data, but new implementation is incurring some performance overhead. You can apply the 20% Rule and ensure that the new timing doesn't exceed 36 seconds to minimize a chance of users perceiving the degradation. However, because the competitor's performance is at 60 seconds, it is possible to breach the 20% and still maintain the relative not-by-much standard by staying under 42 seconds.

QUESTIONABLE DIFFERENTIATION

Mathematically, it is possible for the not-by-much standard to be lower than the 20% cutoff. For example, if one duration is 30 seconds and the other is 35 seconds, the not-by-much standard would be 32 seconds, but 20% of the cutoff is four seconds higher at 36 seconds. This theoretically means that the not-by-much cutoff is not detectable. In this case, if there is evidence that differentiation exists, chances are it is not due to timing differences but rather on factors that are not related to pure timing, such as perception of quality.

Summary

Understanding how users perceive and detect changes in timing helps you define performance objectives. This chapter described two scenarios in terms of D levels (the number of durations involved). For D1 scenarios, where a single duration is involved, the 20% Rule can be applied to setting performance goals and determining regression allowance. For D2 scenarios, in which two durations are involved, the not-by-much standard can be applied to eliminate differentiation by neutralization or to maintain differentiation.

Rabbit Hole

Timing Differences

Hirsh, I. J. (1959). Auditory perception of temporal order. *Journal of the Acoustical Society of America,* 31, 759–767.

Luce, R. D. and E. Galanter. (1963). Discrimination. In R. D. Luce, R. R. Bush, and E. Galanter (Eds.), *Handbook of Mathematical Psychology* (Vol. I, 191–243). New York: Wiley.

Michon, J. A. (1967). *Timing in Temporal Tracking.* Assen, NL: van Gorcum.

Repp, B. H. (2000). Compensation for subliminal timing perturbations in perceptual-motor synchronization. *Psychological Research,* 63, 106–128.

Weber's Law

Ekman, G. (1959). Weber's law and related functions. *The Journal of Psychology, 47,* 343–352.

Fechner, G. T. (1966). *Elements of Psychophysics* (H. E. Adler, Trans.). New York: Holt, Rinehart & Winston. (Original work published 1860.)

Killeen, P. R. and N. A. Weiss (1987). Optimal timing and the Weber Function. *Psychological Review, 94,* 455–468.

Weber, E. H. (1978). *De subtilitate tactus.* (The sense of touch.) In H. E. Ross, D. J. Murray, and J. D. Mollon (Eds.), *The Sense of Touch* (19–138). London: Academic Press. (Original work published 1834.)

Differentiation

Moore, G. (2005). *Dealing with Darwin:* How great companies innovate at every phase of their evolution. New York: Penguin Group.

Geometric Mean Bisection

Alan, L. G. (1991). Human bisection at the geometric mean. *Learning and Motivation,* 22, 39–58.

Church, R. M. and M. Z. Deluty (1977). Bisection of temporal intervals. *Journal of Experimental Psychology: Animal Behavior Processes,* 3, 216–228.

6

Progress Indication

Progress indication is one of the most important topics because it involves one of the most painful human experiences: waiting. Using the wrong type of progress indication can make a seemingly short duration seem unbearable, and using the right type of progress indication can help users tolerate long durations. This chapter introduces a way to classify progress indications and explains how these classes can help you determine the most suitable type of indication to use.

Silicon Faux Pas

When people talk about progress indication, the common imagery that comes to mind is the rotating hourglass or the flying documents, but progress indication is more than some arbitrary animation you use to fill up time. In Chapters 3, "User and System Response Times," and 4, "Responsiveness," I made the analogy between human-computer interaction and human-human conversation. Just as you use nonverbal body language (such as holding up a finger to indicate that you will speak to someone shortly) and verbal expressions (such as the frequent filler words such as *uh* and *um* in midsentence to indicate that you are thinking), progress indication is one of the major and most delicate system-user communication channels. More important, just as there are faux pas in human conversations (such as interrupting someone midsentence or not paying attention during a conversation), there can be violations in progress indications that will be, simply put, plain rude.

Whether you are intrinsically motivated to read this chapter or if you are reading it under duress, chances are you have (1) some form of progress indication, and there is a reason to question whether it is the best one to use, or (2) a particular process in your solution is requiring users to wait, and you want to know what form of progress indication to use, if any at all. Let's start with the situation in which a progress indication already exists in your solution. The first step is to find out what type of progress indication you have by taking the context of the process (download, update, database search, application loading, etc.) into consideration. After you have identified what type or class of progress indication you have, the next step is to design and fine-tune the indication by taking your users into consideration.

Classifying Your Progress Indication

Not all progress indications are created equal. To determine what type of progress indication you already have, you can perform a simple two-part check that I call the *Double Litmus Test* (see Figure 6.1). Imagine taking a screenshot of your progress indication while it is in progress. Can your user reasonably infer from the screenshot how much work or time remains to be done? This might be in work units (such as files found, size of file copied, songs burned, file-size downloaded, percentage of completion, etc.) or in time units (most typically, how much time remaining in seconds, minutes, etc.). If your users can tell or infer how much work or time is remaining, the progress indication is *determinate*, in that users can predict the completion. If your users cannot tell how much work or time remains, your progress indication is described as *indeterminate*.

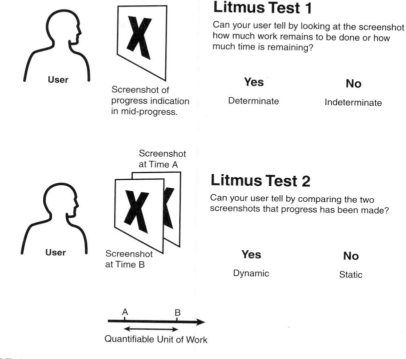

Litmus Test 1

Can your user tell by looking at the screenshot how much work remains to be done or how much time is remaining?

Yes   **No**

Determinate   Indeterminate

Litmus Test 2

Can your user tell by comparing the two screenshots that progress has been made?

Yes   **No**

Dynamic   Static

FIGURE 6.1

The Double Litmus Test: In the first part of the test, if your users can tell how much work or time is left by looking at a screenshot of your progress indication, you have a determinate progress indicator. Otherwise, you have an indeterminate indication. In the second test, if your users can tell the difference between two successive screenshots, you have a dynamic progress indication. Otherwise, you have a static indication.

For the second test, imagine taking a second screenshot after some quantifiable work unit has been done.[1] Any progress that you can determine in code or by some other means can be considered as a work unit. Next, ask whether your users can tell the difference between the first and the second screenshot or if both screenshots look the same. If they can, you have a *dynamic* progress indication because the state of the progress is constantly being updated and displayed to the user. Otherwise, you have a *static* progress indication because users are not given periodic status update. As a footnote, it

[1] If you can't quantify any work units, you can arbitrarily set two points in time during the process, such as two and five minutes into the process.

would be interesting to determine the smallest amount of work unit when users can detect a difference between any two successive screenshots and analyze its timing. Ideally, if you do not want to lose your user's attention, you want the time taken for that amount of work to take no more than seven seconds (at most ten seconds). That is, to deliver some information within successive blocks of time defined by the captive class of responsiveness (Chapter 4). However, for cases when the overall duration is very long (several minutes and longer), it might be better to make sure that the users don't pay attention to the progress indication.

If you have a determinate and dynamic progress indication, you have what I call a *Class A progress indication*. Indications of this class actively provide users with information on how much work or time is remaining before the completion of the process. If your progress indication is indeterminate and static, it falls into the *Class B progress indication,* which is more commonly called "busy" or "working" indication. Usage of these indications should be limited to short processes because users are held hostage to the process without any certainty to when the process will complete. If your progress indication is indeterminate and dynamic, it belongs to *Class C progress indication*. These indications are similar to Class A indications except that they cannot project completion, but they do actively provide users with information about work done or changes in the state of the progress. If your indication is determinate and static, it belongs to the *Class D progress indication*. These indications give some projection of completion, but do not give any information during the process. This is typical of processes that "disappear" into the background and then display a notification upon process completion. Figure 6.2 provides an example for each of these classes.

An easy way to remember these classes is to remember that *A* stands for *active,* in that indication is actively showing remaining work or time units. *B* stands for *busy,* as in indication that the system is busy. *C* stands for *changes* because the indication reports changes in the state of the progress. And *D* stands for *disappear* because the indicator disappears and then appears when the process has completed.

To put these classes into another perspective, imagine visiting a big city for the first time: Class A is like knowing that you have to travel five more city blocks to get to your destination. Class B is the same as not knowing how many blocks you have travelled or how many more you need to travel. Class C is analogous to knowing that you have travelled three blocks, but with no knowledge of your destination. Class D is akin to knowing up front how far the destination is and being informed when you have arrived at the destination. As mentioned at the beginning of this section, no one class is superior to another. Depending on context, one is more suited than the others. In addition, it is possible to use a combination of two or more classes. Which class of progress indication should you use? Read on.

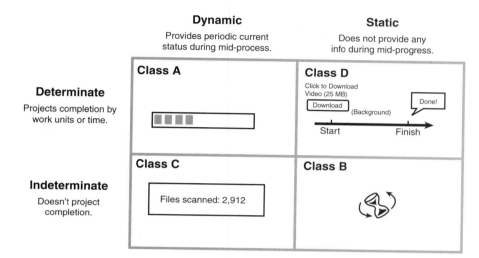

FIGURE 6.2

If the progress indication is dynamic and determinate, it falls into Class A. A progress bar such as the one shown here is an example of such. If the progress indication is static and indeterminate, it falls into Class B. These are the ubiquitous "busy" or "working" indicators. If the progress indicator is dynamic and indeterminate, it falls into Class C. These are like Class A indications without the ability to project completion. If the progress indicator is static and indeterminate, it belongs in Class D. These indicators, such as pop-up notifications, give some sense of completion but do not provide any update until the process has completed.

Choosing the Right Class

In Chapter 4, I gave the first recommendation for progress indication using the continuous class of responsiveness. Specifically, you can use the lower and upper limits of what users expect to be continuous to help you decide whether progress indication is necessary at all. For processes that reliably completes in less than two seconds, there is typically no need to provide any progress indication.

A cautionary note: This recommendation assumes that the process or interaction in question is falling in the right class of responsiveness. A mouse click that triggers a drop-down list, for example, would be more appropriately classified under the instantaneous class. Recall that I mentioned that users understand that the computer needs "thinking time" to perform certain tasks, so a general criterion for the processes applicable to this chapter are the ones perceived to require some computer thinking time. Saving a document, reaching a website, retrieving transaction history, starting an application, and performing a search are great examples.

Beyond two seconds, some form of progress indication is necessary. Between two and five seconds, a simple indication to the user that the system is working is typically sufficient (Class B). The indication can be a typical "busy" animation or a simple line of text that indicates that work is underway, such as "Saving document." Beyond five seconds, it is critical to provide some form of active progress indication to the user (Class A or C). This doesn't mean that the indication cannot take momentary pauses, but it does mean that it must communicate and assure the user that progress is being made. Another class of responsiveness (captive) comes into the picture beyond ten seconds. When a process takes more than ten seconds, you must include an "escape hatch" (typically, a Cancel button) to enable users to abort or ignore the process. For durations reliably beyond five minutes or so, consider providing notification of completion (Class D). I have illustrated these general classes of progress indication and duration cutoffs in Figure 6.3.

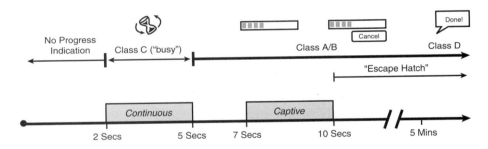

FIGURE 6.3

A diagram to illustrate the application of various classes of progress indication using the responsiveness classes in Chapter 4 as guidance.

Most of your progress indications will involve processes with durations that are either well beyond five seconds or processes that have highly variable and unpredictable durations. Beyond classifying the progress indication to determine the suitability of particular classes of progress indication to particular ranges of durations, in the next section, we take one more step toward designing and tweaking the progress indication.

Designing Your Progress Indication

Put simply, progress indications give users information about the state of a process or interaction, but not all progress indications are created equal. Depending on several factors and context, one form of indication may be better suited than the next. We focus on three essential dimensions that will help you design an optimal progress indication or fine-tune your existing one. Remember that you are not necessarily making binary decisions within each dimension, but more likely you are mixing and matching the various dimensions to suit your user. Think of the classification in the preceding section as deciding whether it is more appropriate to serve breakfast, lunch, or dinner, and think of this section as deciding what exact meal you are going to prepare. The three ingredients to prepare your meal are display modality, progress unit, and data type.

Display Modality: Textual or Visual

The most obvious way to describe a progress indication is to determine whether you are using text, visuals, or a combination of both to communicate progress. Most modern progress indications will likely use both.[2] Many consumer electronics that have limited LCD space typically have text-based progress indication. Others might be more creative in using the LCD screen intended for text to simulate graphics and animation, which is found commonly in non-GUI console, command-line based applications. Visuals include the ubiquitous progress bar, flying documents, rotating hourglass, and so on.

USE TEXTUAL WHEN

- It is important, valuable, or meaningful for the user to know about ongoing processes.
- Users are able and willing to pay attention to read the text.

The obvious value in using text is that it is the best modality for describing the ongoing processes and underlying operations. Therefore, when it is important, valuable, or meaningful to describe the process to the user, text in the progress indication is appropriate. Your user might need to see descriptions of the ongoing process, for example, when mid-failures or mid-processes are meaningful to the user. For instance, a sales representative doesn't need to know the databases, Dynamic Link Library (DLL) files, or any Input/Output (I/O) processes while he is retrieving customer information. A database administrator, on the other hand, might need more description of critical processes, such

---

[2] It is also possible to use auditory indicators, such as the playback of a sound file when the process is complete.

as data backup and so forth. In fact, for critical processes like that, it is common to go beyond displaying descriptive, verbose progress to actually preserving line-by-line progress in a log file.

Text output in a progress indication is useful only if users are able and willing to read the text. Therefore, text should never be used when users are either unable to read because of limited attention span or unwilling to read the words for some other reason. Overall, using text in progress indication is always a good practice; the question is usually how much to use. For Class B indications ("busy" or "working" indications), one or two short meaningful and descriptive words might suffice. Although research shows that people read about four to five words a second, you should keep the number of words to a minimum, preferably just expressing a meaningful verb (or more accurately, as my college English professor would advise, a present participle, such as sav*ing*, load*ing*, etc.). See Figure 6.4 for an idea about how a single process can be expressed in degrees of wordiness.

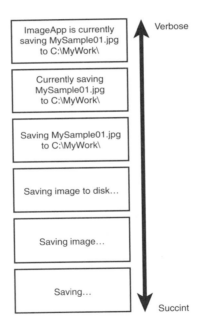

FIGURE 6.4

An example of the degree of how verbose or wordy you can get when describing a simple operation. For mainstream users, keep the text short, preferably with just a present participle (-ing) to indicate what is being done, such as "Saving image" or simply "Saving."

More progress indications than not use messages such as "Please wait," "Stand by," or "One moment please." The terms are typically used when the amount of work or time remaining is indeterminate. Because they do not provide any information during the wait, these terms, by themselves, are really Class B progress indications with text. Therefore, they are more suitable for durations between two and five seconds because the longer a static indication is displayed beyond five seconds, the higher the chance the user will think that the system is hung. When you use Class B progress indications in non-Class B situations, usability and satisfaction issues will eventually arise.

The two possible remedies are to pair the existing indication with an appropriate class or to convert the existing indication to the appropriate class. In both cases, you need to start by (1) asking what work units, objective data, metric, or *any* quantitative or qualitative information can be obtained during the process. Next, you want to (2) describe what type of users you have and what is meaningful to them. The user's relationship to the application and his or her task at hand determines how verbose you need to be. Lastly, you need to (3) determine the right tradeoff between carrying out the process and any overhead incurred in providing feedback. Figure 6.5 describes these steps.

USE VISUAL WHEN

- Details are too technical or meaningless to user.
- Users cannot or will not pay too much attention to the progress indication.

Visuals are excellent when the details are too technical or are meaningless to the user. Many operations within the computer, for example, are too technical for mainstream users. The progress bar is perhaps the most commonly used visual in progress indicators. Graphics and symbols are also suitable when the user's attention span is limited by choice or by the task at hand. A surgeon will probably not want to rely on the text on a strip of LCD on a computer system that is monitoring the vital signs of his or her patient. If the vital signs are at dangerous levels, flashing red lights and loud beeps[3] would be more appropriate. Sometimes, users themselves choose not to pay attention to the progress because they are more interested in the completion of the process than what is happening during the process. In these instances, there is a high likelihood that users will attend to other tasks and occasionally return to the progress indication to see how much progress has been made. Consider, for instance, the following hypothetical scenario:

---

[3] Use of sounds is a perfectly legitimate way to indicate progress. Users with certain disabilities and operators of sensitive and dangerous systems (think pilot in a fighter jet) will also benefit from the use of sounds. However, most mainstream users will be in environments where using sound to indicate progress is not ideal, such as in an office environment or in a public library.

1. Ask what information, metric etc. is obtainable during mid-process...

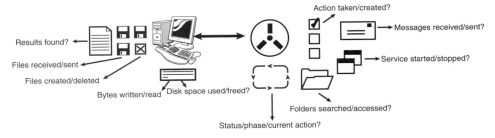

2. Ask what kind of user you have and what is meaningul to them...

3. Decide the trade off between completing process and overhead costs.

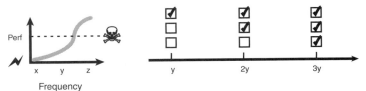

FIGURE 6.5

Many progress indications that contain messages such as "Please Wait" are really Class B ("busy/working") indications with text. Under certain circumstances, however, such as when the duration exceeds more than five seconds, this might be the inappropriate class to use. This diagram illustrates the three steps to rectify this.

A home buyer goes to a real estate website to search for properties, but finds that she needs to install a Java plug-in to view the properties. After clicking a few buttons, she sees a progress bar that suggests that the download has begun. Not wanting to waste time watching the download and installation, she opens another tab in her Web browser to go to another website. About 30 seconds later, she returns to the first website to see whether the download and installation are complete. She quickly spots that the progress bar is less than half filled and immediately swaps over to the second website to continue surfing the Web.

As you can see in this common scenario, the attention devoted to the progress indication is really minute and sporadic because the user is attending to other tasks. Therefore, it is beneficial to use some simple visuals that allow users to understand within a second or two how much progress has been made.

Progress Unit: Time or Work

Another way to describe progress indication is by considering the unit used to communicate the progress. Some progress indications use remaining or elapsed time to communicate progress, whereas others use the number of work units done, being done, or to be done to communicate progress. More commonly, you will find a combination of both time and work units used in progress indications. For example, many applications will display a bit rate (or bitrate), such as 128 kbps, which really expresses an amount of work (kb or kilobits) in a fixed time unit (s or seconds).

USE TIME UNITS WHEN

- You can confidently project completion time.
- Users are anxious to consume what comes upon completion.
- Users will likely work on other tasks while waiting for completion.
- Some communication with another live party is involved.

Time units come in two flavors: remaining time and elapsed time. In only a handful of instances is reporting elapsed time valuable, and so this section focuses on reporting remaining time. Instances when elapsed time proves useful almost always involve one or more meaningful actions that the user can take because a certain amount of time has passed. This may be true in some messaging and communication applications when it is good for the user to know that the other party has not responded, so that the user can resend a message or take other appropriate actions. Another situation when reporting elapsed time is potentially valuable is when performance or diagnostic measurements are critical. There are some instances when time elapsed is used simply because the process is indeterminate. This is not a good practice because it literally provides users with a means to quantify the wait. Imagine a hostess of a restaurant coming up to you every five minutes to tell you how long you have waited for your table! Once again, unless the user needs to take one or more actions because a certain amount of time has gone by, report remaining time rather than elapsed time.

Time units should be used only when you can project the completion time fairly accurately. In addition, time units are optimal when users are focused on what is after the completion of the process because no one likes to wait; knowing that the wait is getting shorter, however, alleviates the agony of waiting. Besides functioning to pacify impatient users, time remaining helps users gauge how much time they can devote to other tasks, such as switching to another application, grabbing a coffee, or going to lunch.

Two cautionary notes about reporting time units:

- You need to be careful about how the time units are expressed. This is discussed in Chapter 7, "Expressing Time," but for now note that reporting a second-by-second time-remaining countdown might lead to the same suboptimal experience as a time-elapsed counter. Time anchors (1, 2, 3, 5, 10, 15, 20, 30) and ranges (such as five to ten minutes) create a better experience in most cases than if you use the exact time remaining (such as 8:30 minutes).

- Time units should either remain unchanged momentarily or decrease. They should never increase. Incrementing remaining time is oxymoronic and understandably described as moronic by users. This phenomenon, by no means infrequent, typically occurs when the projected completion time is dynamically calculated based on remaining workload (such as number of files copied, folders to search, etc.) factoring in available resources such as processing power, memory, bandwidth, and so forth. Because the time units are yoked together in a mathematical equation with the resource, any hiccup or stalling in the resource upsets the equation and is manifested as additional time costs, thereby increasing the remaining time (see Figure 6.6). J. C. Dvorak describes this as the Time-Fluctuation Phenomenon in one of his commentaries in *PC Magazine*: "Okay, it's a big folder, so you decide to go downstairs to watch some TV. The copying begins. It looks good. In fact, it's going pretty fast. Then the time drops to two hours! Then it jumps to three hours! Then back to two hours and ten minutes! What's so difficult about estimating the time?"

There are a few possible remedies for the Time-Fluctuation Phenomenon. Ideally, if the computing resource can be reserved to perform the task, the projected remaining time will be steady and not increment or fluctuate. This is not always possible because computing resources such as a central processing unit (CPU) and memory can be shared by many other processes. A more possible fix is to unyoke the time units from the computing resource (or any resource that may be subject to high variability) in the calculation, and report the time remaining as a range based on high and low computing resource. Another practice is to give users an idea about the available resource along with the remaining time units to build user tolerance.[4] This approach is often used for

[4] This is also an effective technique that in essence shifts the "blame" to the user's hardware, such that users are aware that their hardware is a limiting factor.

large downloads from the Internet (where the bit rate is specified) and when connecting over a wireless network (where the signal strength and speeds are specified). If these fixes are not possible, you might want to consider the other progress unit: work units.

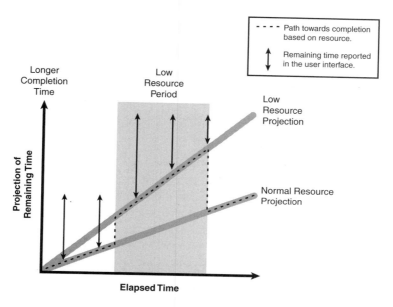

FIGURE 6.6

This diagram illustrates the Time-Fluctuation Phenomenon. Under normal resource availability, the projected remaining time will continue to decrease. However, if the resources are momentarily limited (such as when another process is being instantiated), the completion time is recalculated and the projected remaining time will suddenly increase. What the users see as a result is the remaining-time estimates fluctuating.

USE WORK UNITS WHEN

- Remaining time is too variable or unpredictable.
- Users are involved in setting up the steps in the process.
- Mid-progress failures are meaningful and actionable to the user.

As mentioned in the preceding section, when the remaining time is susceptible to fluctuations, work units might prove a better alternative. The top of Figure 6.5 shows some examples of work units. Another general rule of thumb is to use work units when it is meaningful or valuable to the user to know about the work that has been completed, the current work being done, or the work that is left to be done. One instance when this is true is when users are somehow involved in setting or customizing the steps in the process. Watching the steps completed ensures users that the steps have been correctly performed. One great example is burning songs onto a CD; when you see the successful completion of each song, you have a certain degree of assurance that the process is progressing as expected. Another instance when it is useful to see work units is when responses to mid-progress failure are necessary or meaningful, especially when the failures do not halt the entire process.

There a few important things to remember about using work units. First, work units do not necessarily always mean the exact byte being written, actual files being copied, or the current folder being searched. They can also include the phase of the installation, the action completed, and so on. In addition, work units can be expressed as either a percentage, such as "35% of video downloaded," or some actual aggregate value, such as "3 of 5 files downloaded." Second, it is always possible to build in layers of information that becomes increasingly more detailed and specific if and when users choose to reveal the next layer. This is called *progressive disclosure*. If you include layers of information, starting with the abstract, users who do not care about or understand the nitty-gritty details will not be bombarded and overloaded by what they see. Users who are more advanced can choose to disclose more advanced information. Figure 6.7 illustrates this simple but powerful technique.

Data Type: Quantitative or Qualitative

A third way to describe progress indication is to determine whether the information presented ought to be quantitative or qualitative. A quantitative data type has a numeric value in the time or work units, such as "About 30 minutes remaining" or "Downloaded 3MB of 12MB." A qualitative data type typically expresses some state, phase, or property of the progress, such as "Removing temporary files."

USE QUANTITATIVE DATA WHEN

- Users need objective data to analyze failure, performance, or other diagnostics.
- It will provide assurance that work units have successfully completed.

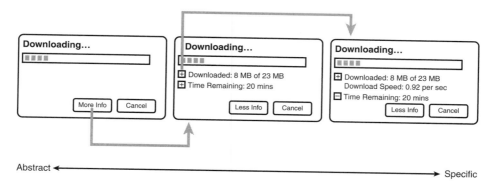

FIGURE 6.7

This diagram explains the concept of progressive disclosure. Upon starting, no specific details are shown. Users who are savvier may then choose to disclose more information (in this case, by clicking on the More Info button). If knowing the download speed is meaningful or valuable to the user, he or she can choose to see that by expanding the tree node. The idea here is to manage information in such a way to accommodate both mainstream and advanced users.

Display quantitative data when users need objective data. Such data proves especially helpful to users who need to analyze a failure, measure performance, or perform some other diagnostic task. Case in point: Cyclic redundancy check (CRC) in file and data management. CRC is an error-detection technique used to ensure that the file is faithfully transmitted. If you are not familiar with CRC, think of it as an invoice that states how many items should be found in the shipment. When you receive the shipment, you want to verify that the actual number of items and the numbers shown on the invoice matches. If the numbers don't match, something is wrong. Likewise in the transmission of a file, CRC ensures that the data read from the source is the data written to the destination. Errors in reading and writing data to CDs and DVDs, for instance, are frequently related to CRC failures. Imagine a mainstream user burning songs onto a CD and seeing a seemingly endless and meaningless string of numbers spat out by the CRC algorithm during the reading and writing of each song; this would not be meaningful to the user. All that needs to be communicated to the user in this instance is just some simple visuals to indicate the number of songs burned onto the CD and the status of the burning.

Uncertainty amplifies the pain of waiting. The display of quantitative data can sometimes provide some assurance that things are progressing correctly, even if users might not entirely understand the operations. Case in point: antivirus scanning. Although mainstream users probably do not need to know which exact file is being scanned (unless there is an action to take, such as when an infected file is found), being able to see a running number or a progress bar that increments with each file or groups of files being scanned provides some level of assurance that the antivirus application is doing its job. This is a great example of Class C progress indication in action. You don't know when it is going to finish (indeterminate), but you know that it's working (dynamic). As a reminder, do not forget that you can use progressive disclosure here, too.

USE QUALITATIVE DATA WHEN

- Quantitative data is meaningless to the user.
- Users benefit from reading a simple description of work done.
- There is a mid-progress need to call something to the user's attention.

One of the uses for qualitative data is to simplify work units into phases. This proves useful when the actual work units are meaningless to the user. For example, instead of telling users that 251 setup files and 36 support files have been copied into four folders in a temporary folder, it might be better just to say that all the setup files have been successfully copied. Thus, qualitative data is great to summarize aggregate work completed. Many operations are too technical for users, such as the CRC example mentioned previously, but knowing the stages might be useful and assuring. Suppose, for instance, you have a contractor periodically reporting to you the number of screws and hinges used in your kitchen remodeling. Qualitative data, in this example, would be like having the contractor inform you that the cabinets are all done and that he is moving on to the countertop.

Qualitative data is also appropriate when there is a need to call an issue to the user's attention. Some motherboard manufacturers, such as Intel, build sensors throughout the motherboard to monitor its operating temperature because overheating can cause irreversible damage. The manufacturers might provide a software application[5] (Intel has one called Active Monitor) that displays the actual temperature (quantitative) including some qualitative display, such as a red blinking "Motherboard is overheating!" would definitely catch the user's attention a lot better.

---

[5] Many motherboard manufacturers include this functionality, but the temperature reading is buried in the BIOS setup utility application that is usually only accessible (by pressing a designated function key and sometimes supplying a password) during the first few seconds of the computer booting. How do you like that for discoverability and accessibility?

Summary

This chapter introduced the four classes of progress indication: Class A for determinate and dynamic indications, Class B for indeterminate and static indications, Class C for indeterminate and dynamic indications, and Class D for determinate and static indications. You can fine-tune these progress indicators by choosing the appropriate display modality (textual/visual), progress units (time/work), and data type (quantitative/qualitative).

Rabbit Hole

Progress Indications

Apple Developer Connection (2006). *Indicators*. (Author's note: You can find an online version at http://developer.apple.com/documentation/UserExperience/Conceptual/OSXHIGuidelines/XHIGControls/chapter_18_section_5.html.)

Johnson, J. (2000). *GUI Bloopers: Don'ts and Do's for Software Developers and Web Designers.* San Diego, CA: Academic Press. (Author's note: See Chapter 7.)

McInerney, P. and J. Li (2002). *Progress indication: Concepts, design, and implementation. IBM developerWorks*. (Author's note: You can find an online version at www.ibm.com/developerworks/library/us-progind/.)

Myers, B. A. (1985). *Importance of percent-done progress indicators for computer-human interfaces.* CHI '85 Proceedings. ACM.

Time-Fluctuation Phenomenon

Dvorak, D. C. (2007). Windows' words of doom. *PC Magazine* (May 2). (Author's note: You can find an online version at www.pcmag.com/article2/0,1759,2123848,00.asp.)

Progressive Disclosure

Fowler, S. and V. Stanwick (2004). *Web application design handbook: Best practices for Web-based software.* San Francisco: Morgan Kaufmann Publishers. (Author's note: See page 157 for progressive disclosure.)

Hmelo-Silver, C. and H. S. Barrows (2006). Goals and strategies of a problem-based learning facilitator. *Interdisciplinary Journal of Problem-based Learning,* 1, 21–39. (Author's note: Progressive disclosure applied outside of human-computer interaction.)

Nielsen, J. (2006). *Progressive Disclosure.* Jakob Nielsen's Alertbox (December 4). (Author's note: You can find the online version at www.useit.com/alertbox/progressive-disclosure.html.)

7

Expressing Time

In many instances, especially in progress indications, you need to communicate to your user some aspect of time, such as remaining time or estimated completion time. Although it may seem trivial and superficial, how you express time in the user interface (UI) can determine how your user experiences and perceives your solution. Simple words—for good or bad—can alter perception and affect tolerance. This chapter discusses when and how you should express time in the UI of your solution and introduces the use of time anchors.

The Timing of Time: Past, Present, Future

Besides *what* you express (phrases, time units, etc.) and *how* you express it (text, graphical, etc.), you also need to consider *when* you provide timing information to your user. For example, telling a person who is about to stand in line how long it will take to get to the front of the line has a different effect and serves a different purpose than informing the person who is already standing halfway in the line. Simply put, when you release information can make or break an experience. We all have our share of horror stories of how the mistiming of some information, sometimes by a matter of mere seconds, changed the course of events.

Users will use any information revealed by the UI—by design or otherwise—to form a perception of an interaction or process. This shouldn't be a surprise because we all do something similar every day. We make predictions based on patterns we see (long lines equal long wait), evaluate the quality of things based on signs and symptoms (blemishes equal carelessness), and form theories about why things happen the way they did (broken because of poor-quality parts). Likewise, users will use *any* timing information to help them understand and decide how they feel about and respond to the duration of an interaction.

Consider the following questions:

- How long will this take?
- How much longer will this take?
- How much time did that take?

Each of these three questions relates to a different temporal perspective; that is, where you are in temporal relation to some event. We can perceive durations from three basic temporal perspectives. First, we can anticipate, set expectations, or predict the duration of an event before it begins. Because the event has not happened, we'll describe this as *prospective*. In the UI, informing users how long a download will take, for example, is giving users a prospective estimate of the duration of the download. Second, we assess the duration of an event in *real time* while it is transpiring. A great example is reporting remaining time as the download is progressing. Finally, we can also evaluate the duration after event has transpired. We describe this last one as *retrospective*. Telling users how much time the download took after it has completed is an example. As mentioned, *when* you provide information about the duration of some event can influence user perception and shape user experience. Let's take a closer look at each of the perspectives.

Prospective: Tickle-Me-Elmo

It is not immediately intuitive that perception can be established, let alone be affected, before the actual experience. The key factor in prospective assessments is that a certain degree of judgment may have already been passed before the actual experience. If the judgment is negative, people can be hesitant in proceeding because they are, in essence, predicting that the experience will not match up or meet up to their expectation. An inordinate number of factors can go into forming or influencing the perception of a solution. In the retail industry, it is commonly known that people choose not to buy, use, or even try a specific solution based on its association, reputation, brand, or even price (not necessarily too expensive, but also too cheap!). On the flip-side, for the same reasons, people will go through hell and high water to get their hands on a product. In 1996, for instance, marketing hype and demand for the then-new Tickle-Me-Elmo dolls fueled fights among Christmas shoppers, some of whom reportedly paid upward of $1,500 for the $30 doll.

REPORT TIME PROSPECTIVELY WHEN

- Users need to decide if they can "afford" to start the process.
- Users would likely want to attend to other tasks.
- The process is very long or captive.

Keep in mind that most users do not devote their entire time and undivided attention to using your solution. More likely, users will have a few applications running, not to mention other active noncomputing tasks happening (talking to a customer on the phone, watching TV, etc.). Users, like computers, are efficient multitaskers. To a great extent, the mental gymnastics they have to perform to attend to several tasks simultaneously is desirable because it translates to productivity and proficiency: "While the file is downloading, let me find that e-mail Marketing sent me so that we can look at it together while we are on the phone."

Any process that hijacks or compromises the user's ability to multitask will break the user's flow and experience. Imagine if the file download requires a dial-up connection that runs on the same phone line or if the e-mail program is hogging so much network bandwidth that the file download is halted or significantly slowed down. Therefore, give users an estimate of how much time so that they can decide whether they can afford to start or engage the process (see Figure 7.1). Examples of these include instances when the process is very time-consuming or captive—that is, when the process will commandeer some level of the application, operating system, or the entire computer system such that users have to wait out the process before proceeding.

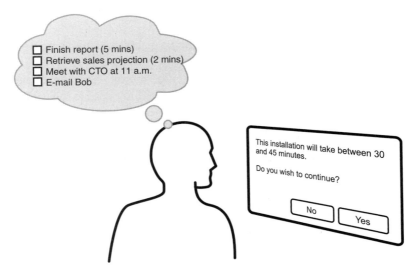

FIGURE 7.1

When time estimates are reported to the users prospectively, it allows users to decide whether they can afford to proceed with the process without breaking user flow or compromising other priorities.

Real Time: Scratch-and-Sniff

Perception obviously changes moment to moment as more information about something becomes available as it is being experienced. The retail world learned a long time ago that getting people to experience some product or service (by sight, touch, taste, smell, or sound) is one of the most powerful marketing techniques because perception built through direct experience is lasting compared to perception built vicariously through commercials and ads. This gave birth to the world of free samples, movie trailers, trial memberships, 30-day trial software, test drives, model homes, and Scratch-and-Sniff stickers. Although these work before the actual experience, they give consumers a taste, or better, a promise of the full experience. There is a flip-side to having real-time information, too. When the actual experience is not what was promised or expected, informed consumers will want to bail out. That gave birth to the world of refunds, money-back guarantees, and store credits!

REPORT TIME IN REAL TIME WHEN

- Ongoing processes and operations are too technical or meaningless to the user.
- There is a need for users to know and act on elapsed time.

Giving users real-time information about an ongoing process was the distinctive feature behind the Class A and C progress indications mentioned in Chapter 6, "Progress Indication." Providing remaining time, for example, typically provides assurance that progress is being made and progressively informs users that the wait is getting shorter. When detail about what is being done (work units) is too technical or meaningless to the user, show remaining time rather than remaining work. For example, detail about a few files being copied from one folder to another may be meaningful to mainstream users, but detail about a few hundred files being copied from the installation DVD to a temporary folder is not. Therefore, showing files copied in the former case may be acceptable, but showing time remaining might be better in the latter case. Figure 7.2 shows another example of hiding what is not meaningful and only showing what is meaningful in the UI.

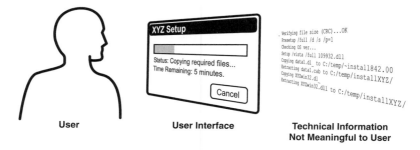

User User Interface **Technical Information Not Meaningful to User**

FIGURE 7.2

When detail about the process is too technical or meaningless to the user, report estimated remaining time to the user in real time.

Providing elapsed time is another way to provide real-time information, but to reiterate an important point, report elapsed time with care. As a rule of thumb, elapsed time should be used only when it is meaningful for the user to see it, such as for diagnostic purposes and performance evaluation. As a footnote, not displaying elapsed time doesn't mean not tracking elapsed time. Prompting users for actions when waits become usually long is a good idea when tracking elapsed time is useful.

Retrospective: Worst Episode Ever!

It is natural for people to evaluate a product or service after experiencing it (like the comic book guy in *The Simpsons* whose catch phrase is "Worst episode ever!") Thankfully, research has shown that it is possible to negate some ill effects of long waits with compelling value or highly desirable outcomes, particularly with great service.

Understanding how people look back at an experience is critical because there is a high likelihood that they will repeat or reengage the same experience if they found it enjoyable. Repeating or returning to what was deemed rewarding is a basic principle called Law of Effect. Beyond returning or repeating the experience, people also become pro bono marketing mouthpieces if the experience was positive (so called word-of-mouth marketing or WOMM) or a vitriolic critic if the experience was negative. In this modern age of blogs, ensuring that people look back at an experience and evaluate it positively is even more important.

REPORT TIME RETROSPECTIVELY WHEN

- It is meaningful or valuable for users to know how long a process took.
- Diagnostic measurement or performance assessments is necessary.

Reporting elapsed time retrospectively (after a process has been completed) should be done only when it is meaningful or valuable for the user to know how long a process has taken, such as during diagnostic measurements or performance assessments (see Figure 7.3). For most mainstream applications, there is little value in telling users how much time was taken. If there is any doubt, fill in the blank: "My users will use the reported elapsed time to _____." Other than "tell how time has elapsed," whatever you can fill in the blank should reflect your users, their needs, and how they use your solution. If you cannot fill in the blank, reporting elapsed time might very well be a bad idea in your solution.

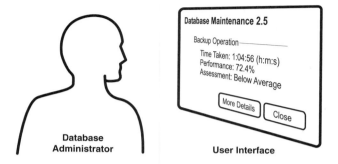

Database Administrator

User Interface

FIGURE 7.3

Report time elapsed retrospectively only when it is valuable for users to see the amount of time taken to complete the process. This diagram illustrates an example of a database administrator viewing the output of a maintenance program that informs the administrator whether the performance of the maintenance was acceptable.

Talking Time

To drink eight glasses of water every day is a recommendation some people heed religiously. The idea here is that there are health benefits, such as preventing dehydration, by simply drinking around eight glasses of water every day. This recommendation is simple until one starts to get technical about the volumetric quantity of glasses. Of course, the idea in using "glasses" is that it is easy and more practical to express than ounces or milliliters. Other than contexts in which precision is critical, such as brain surgery or aerospace engineering, for most parts of our lives we do not use or need precise measurements because estimations suffice. Perception is often inaccurate, and for most activities in life and work, it doesn't need not be. In day-to-day activities, we often rely on common objects when estimating and expressing quantity: The meatball was about the size of a golf ball. The new credit card-size digital camera is for sale next month. This way of speaking is common for estimating volume, mass, distance, and so forth.

For estimation of time, we are more likely to use proper time units (seconds, minutes, hours) instead of using references to objects or events. For example, not many people (at least in the Western culture) will state that they waited for table at a restaurant for about four to five times the amount of time it takes to boil an egg, or that the food took about 50 Hail Marys to be served. One possible instance of when we do not use proper time units is when we compare one duration with another. For example, "By the time we got our table, we could have finished dinner at the other restaurant." Nevertheless, we're prone to simplify the estimation of time as we do for the estimation of other measures.

Time Anchors

Think about your last meaningful conversation with someone. How long did the conversation last? If you have to use time units such as seconds and minutes, there is a high likelihood that you will use whole numbers, like 1, 2, 5, or 10, to describe the duration. When we are asked to characterize durations of trivial events, we seldom give precise estimates such as 10.7 seconds or 5.17 minutes unless we are deliberately clocking the duration with a stopwatch or a wristwatch. Instead, we gravitate toward particular numbers to estimate durations. I call these *time anchors* because people tend to anchor their estimation to one or more of these numbers (see Figure 7.4). The term *anchor* is used to highlight the fact that although we know that an event lasted less than or more than five minutes, we still gravitate toward five when we have to verbalize an estimation.

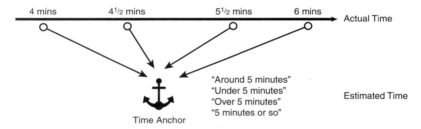

FIGURE 7.4

Although the average person can detect differences between two durations, the tendency is to use time anchors to give time estimates.

To illustrate the effects of time anchors, consider that following statements:

- The conversation with my manager lasted no more than five minutes.
- He got up to the stage and froze for about 30 seconds.
- He was more than ten minutes late for the meeting.

Now consider how odd it is if these statements did not use time anchors:

- The conversation with my manger lasted no more than 4.3 minutes.
- He got up to the stage and froze for about 34 seconds.
- He was more than 9.44 minutes late for the meeting.

Using precise units (in contexts that are trivial, casual, noncritical, or colloquial) gives the impression that the given time estimates are exact, which either leads people to trustingly assume that you timed the event or invites them to verify the accuracy of the estimates given. If you know that your conversation with your manager lasted for 4.3 minutes, chances are you weren't paying attention, were you?

Time Anchor Matrix

For time estimations under a few hours, people tend to gravitate toward the numbers 1, 2, 3, 5, 10, 15, 20, and 30. That is, when asked to estimate a short duration, people are prone to using one or more numbers, such as "about ten seconds" or "two to three minutes," in their estimates. This is observable for durations in the magnitude of hours, but to a lesser extent. A quick way to remember these numbers is to express them in what I have called a *Time Anchor Matrix* (see Figure 7.5).

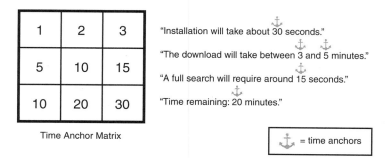

Time Anchor Matrix

FIGURE 7.5

The numbers toward which people gravitate when expressing time can be easily remembered in the Time Anchor Matrix.

The average person can tell the difference between four minutes and eight minutes, so the matrix doesn't imply that we are only capable of estimating time using these whole numbers, or that we perceive everything in the world in chunks of time dictated by these numbers. Rather, it suggests that these are easy and practical numbers we are comfortable and confident using when we have to describe the length of time, particularly in impromptu and trivial contexts.

Why people gravitate toward these numbers is not clear, but it is highly likely that our sexagesimal (base-60) clock system has a strong influence. Another obvious influence is language and culture. In certain parts of the world, quantifying time in seconds and minutes is not typical. In some Muslim countries, time is commonly expressed relative to the five daily Muslim prayers. In Israel, time is commonly expressed relative to an hourly news broadcast.

Talking Time

Just as humans discovered that they can communicate with aliens in musical notes in Steven Spielberg's *Close Encounters with the Third Kind* or in mathematical languages in the late Carl Sagan's novel *Contact*, we can use the Time Anchor Matrix to communicate time estimates to the user. The three main flavors of time estimation are ranges, limits, and countdowns.

RANGES: BETWEEN X AND Y

Time anchors come in handy when there is a need to specify a range of times to represent the possible durations of an event. This happens frequently when one or more other factors can influence the variability of the duration. For example, if we are confident that a particular process will take around four minutes, we can state (display in the UI) a range that spans over four minutes. Referring to the Time Anchor Matrix, we see that 3 and 5 are the integers that are the two surrounding candidates, and therefore we state that the process will take between three and five minutes (see Figure 7.6).

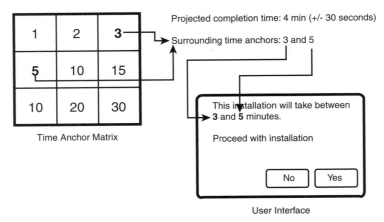

FIGURE 7.6

An example of how to use the Time Anchor Matrix to express a range of durations in the UI.

A rule of thumb for specifying ranges is not to skip over any successive time anchor. For example, we don't want to state 5 to 15 minutes because that skips over 10. The reason for not using wide ranges can be illustrated with a little imagination: Compare your response to the promise of two hypothetical cable companies, one promising that their service technician will be at your residence between 10 a.m. and 12 p.m., and the other stating that their technician will be there between 10 a.m. and 3 p.m. When the difference between two time anchors is too large, we begin to feel that the range could reasonably be tighter. Why a wide range would cause annoyance is possibly tied to a classic psychophysical principle called the Weber-Fechner Law that was mentioned in Chapter 5, "Detecting Timing Differences." Without going into detail, it is likely that using successive numbers theoretically makes it more difficult for people to perceive and "insert" one or more time anchors in between the high and low ends of the range.

LIMITS: LESS THAN OR MORE THAN X

There are two ways to express time limits, and each serves very different purposes. Lower limits tell users that a particular duration will take at least X amount of time. Upper limits tell users that a particular duration will not take more than X amount of time. You should use lower limits with care because it is essentially a warning of inevitable wait, and such statements are typically made to brace an individual for the wait or delay: *The road trip to Vancouver will take at least three hours. The package will take at least one week to get to Singapore. The house inspection will take more than two hours.* In contrast, an upper limit is a guarantee of completion: *You will reach Vancouver by midnight. You will receive the package within the month. The house inspection will be done in one hour.* Lower limits warn, and upper limits promise.

When it is not possible or wise to state a range, use the latter to state the longest possible duration in a statement such as "less than five minutes." When stating upper limits, round up to the next element in the Time Anchor Matrix. For example, if we are confident that a particular process will be completed in 7 minutes and 50 seconds, we'll state that the process will take under 10 minutes. Use the former when there is a need to warn users prospectively that a process will take a long time, especially if it is captive process when users cannot interact with parts of the application, operating system, or the entire machine until the process is completed. These are instances when you have some confidence that it will definitely take at least a certain amount of time. In such cases, state lower limits and do likewise in rounding up to the next highest time anchor. For example, if a process will take at least 3 minutes and 45 seconds, inform users that the process will take at least 5 minutes (see Figure 7.7). Underpromise and overdeliver.

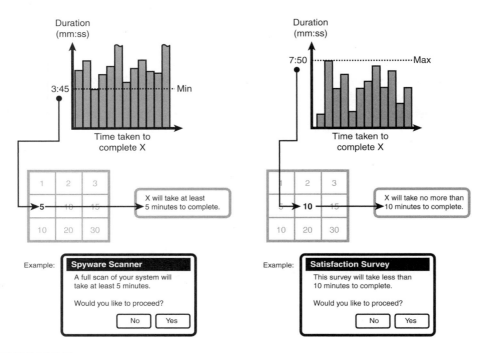

FIGURE 7.7

Two illustrations of how lower limits (left) and upper limits (right) are used. Lower limits warn user of unavoidable wait, which functions to help users decide whether they can proceed with the process (spyware scanning, for example). Upper limits guarantee that a process will complete by a certain time, and thus functions well as a persuasive mechanism to encourage users to proceed.

The argument against using specific and precise numbers, such as 7 minutes and 50 seconds or even 8 minutes, is that when we use numbers that users are not accustomed to using (that is, numbers not represented by the Time Anchor Matrix), we risk making them hold us to what we apparently promised. This expectation is likely due to the fact that your statement is construed as one that has been made after rigorous timing and performance testing and that you have somehow locked down eight minutes with precision. In contrast, when you use the next higher integer in the matrix, ten minutes, it will more likely be perceived as a rough estimation because the colloquial prevalence of "ten minutes."

REMAINING TIME: Z, Y, H...

Unless there is a compelling need to report elapsed time (0:01…0:02…0:03…), it is always better to use a time-remaining or count-down timer (0:54…0:53…0:52…) if there is any need to show a timer at all. Reserve such use of timers to relatively shorter durations that are around ten minutes and shorter. Imagine watching a count-down timer from one hour: 1:00:00…0:59:59…0:59:58…0:59:57…. Obviously this would be too frustrating to watch!

Because a time-elapsed timer decrements like a clock or a stopwatch, providing it alongside a lengthy process is equivalent to inviting users to time the process, which will increase the chances of shooting yourself in the foot. Although the use of time-remaining timers is relatively and generally better, if the countdown is set to "tick" by the second, it can have the same adverse effect as a time-elapsed timer. This is where the time anchors come in handy. Instead of specifying every single second between 10 minutes and 0 seconds (10:00…9:59…9:59…9:58…), for example, express the countdown in time anchor units: (10 minutes…5 minutes…3 minutes…2 minutes…1 minute…30 seconds…).

As a footnote, when reporting remaining time, never allow remaining time to increase. At most, remaining time can remain unchanged momentarily, but it should never get longer, or worse, fluctuate. If your remaining time is prone to fluctuations, making remaining time difficult to predict, remaining time might not be the best progress unit to use.

Couple of Whiles

Sometimes stating ranges or upper limits is not possible because the estimated time depends on factors that are too variable or too difficult to predict. One notorious example is accessing a resource such as a database over the network. Even if the network connection speed can be determined, factors beyond the connection speed can adversely affect the access to the database. The dilemma of not being able to predict how long something will last and the need to provide some time estimate commonly leads to the use of phrases such as "a few moments," "please wait," or "a while." This practice might not be the best approach because such phrases are highly ambiguous and do not provide users with any certainty or comfort about the process.

Time and timing-related terms, such as "a few moments" or "a while," can be problematic because they are subjectively perceived and heavily dependent on context, not to mention culture, language, age, and so forth. That is, it is unlikely that such terms are quantified and perceived similarly from one person to the next, between the service provider and the consumer, and between us and the recording on the phone that keeps promising that that someone will be with us "momentarily." The pain of being put on hold on the phone for a seemingly indefinite time really stems from *uncertainty,* and the cure then is to provide some certainty.

As an example, the customer service departments in some companies make it a practice to have staff answer a phone call as it comes but quickly inform the caller that she will be put on hold: "ABC company, can you hold please?" This practice works to a certain degree because it provides some *certainty* to the user that he or she has probably dialed the right number and has at least reached a live person on the line. Likewise, the user benefits from some certainty about *any* work being done even if a time estimate is not possible. The following are some remedies and implementations to consider in lieu of using ambiguous terms:

1. Give Non-temporal Information

The first remedy is to treat this issue as a progress indication. When the completion of the process cannot be projected and no status is available to the user, we essentially have a Class B scenario (see Figure 6.2) or a Busy/Working indication. Therefore, we want to do the exercise described in Figure 6.5 to find a way to move this to the lower-bottom quadrant to make it a Class C progress indication. In other words, we want to find all possible information and display the meaningful ones to the user (such as numbers of lines read, number of projects searched, updated queue information, compiling phase, etc.) as the process is ongoing.

2. Timers and Timeout

Although the elapsed time typically should not be used in the UI, it can be used under the covers to implement a mechanism that will respond to abnormal delays. This is found in many telecommunication devices, such as cell phones when the device will stop ringing after a fixed number of rings or a fixed amount of time. In the software world, we typically find such timeout mechanism in Internet browsers or some network-related solutions. The key in implementing this is to determine what actions to take at what time. The first step is to use data or models to map out the distribution of latencies and associate them with success and failure rates. For example, you might find that beyond 30 seconds of inactivity, failure rates are at 90%. In this case, you might want to provide a means for the user to continue, abandon, or restart the process when a delay goes beyond 30 seconds. As a relevant footnote, beyond ten seconds (captive class, see Chapter 4, "Responsiveness"), an "escape hatch," such as a Cancel or Retry button, is highly recommended.

Time Grammar and Etiquette

You should observe a few simple rules when expressing time in the UI. You will find more techniques and violations in later chapters, but here are five immediate ones to pay attention to.

1. Singularize Singular Units

It is always good practice to write the extra few lines of code to ensure that the time units are appropriately singular when necessary. For example, "1 minutes" should be "1 minute," and "1 seconds" should be "1 second." If you need to display time units that are smaller than one, use plurals, as in "0 seconds" or "0.5 minutes." (A better expression for "0 seconds" would be with a term such as *complete* or *done*.) A way to remember when to use singular units is to remember that singulars are used for exactly one, no more and no less.

2. Zero Means Finished!

In reporting remaining time, "0 seconds" implies that the process is complete and therefore should not reflect any more ongoing process. Sometimes, another process kicks in after the first process has completed, such as the unpacking of a downloaded file. What the users see, however, is a process that appears to be perpetually almost done but never does finish. The remedy is to either inform users what new process has begun or include the time needed by the extra processes into the remaining time estimates.

3. Express Time Units Consistently

The common practice is to express time units numerically, such as "This installation will take 1 to 2 minutes." It is possible to express in words, such as "one to two minutes" but never mix the two ("one to 2 minutes"). Double-digit time units are better expressed numerically, such as "15 minutes" as opposed to verbally "fifteen minutes."

4. Between X and Y

When the preposition *between* is used, make sure the conjunction *and* is used, too, as in "This installation will taken between three *and* five minutes" not "This installation will taken between three *to* five minutes." Using *to* as in "This installation will take one *to* two minutes" is fine.

5. Avoid Ambiguous Phrases

Use of the phrases *momentarily* or *a while* might be lead to more user annoyance than not. Do not use these ambiguous terms just because a process has unpredictable completion time. Refer to Chapter 6 and consider the right class of progress indication to use. The term *second* in "We'll be with you in a second," is extremely overused and is not taken as literally as it reads. An informal survey showed that the median expectation of "a second" was around six seconds, whereas "a minute" and "an hour" are likely to be taken more literally. Adjectives and adverbs, such as *immediately* and *instantly,* are also ambiguous.

Summary

When timing information is expressed in the UI is as important as how to express it. Whether information is shown prospectively, in real time or retrospectively can significantly influence user's perception, behavior, and experience. This chapter provided some guidance for expressing time. In expressing time units, use time anchors to express ranges, limits, and remaining time to prevent users from thinking that estimations are exact. Some time expression grammatical rules and etiquette are also spelled out, such as singularizing singular units.

Rabbit Hole

Prospective Versus Retrospective Time

Teigen, K. H. and K. I. Karevold (2005). Looking back versus looking ahead: Framing of time and work at different stages of a project. *Journal of Behavioral Decision Making,* 18, 229–246.

Underestimation and Overestimation of Prospective Time

Roy, M. M., N. J. S. Christenfeld, and C. R. M. McKenzie (2005). Underestimating the duration of future events memory: Incorrectly used or memory bias. *Psychological Bulletin,* 131, 738–756.

Zauberman, G. and J. G. Lynch (2005). Resource slack and propensity to discount delayed investments of time versus money. *Journal of Experimental Psychology: General,* 134, 23–37.

Writing Styles

The Chicago Manual of Style Online. (Author's note: Available online at www.chicagomanualofstyle.org/indexT.html. Various guidance under "Time.")

Anchors and Estimation of Time

Konig, C. J. (2005). Anchors distort estimates of expected duration. *Psychological Reports, 96,* 253–256.

8

User Flow

How "smooth" and enjoyable users find your solution can often be described as the *user flow*. A user flow that is not optimal can feel like an eternity to the users as they get dragged through each painful step. Conversely, an optimal user flow can help with time-consuming tasks because users may not notice the passing time. Even if they are aware of the time that has gone by, they might even actually enjoy every moment of it. This chapter discusses how to ensure an optimal user flow using concepts borrowed from research in the psychology of flow.

What Is User Flow?

In Chapter 2, "Perception and Tolerance," we talked about how perception and perceived time can be underestimated or overestimated. In short, design "violations" can cause short durations to feel longer than they really are, and conversely, carefully applied techniques can make long durations feel shorter than they really are. Similarly, bad design can make short durations difficult to tolerate, and optimal design can make long durations tolerable. How perception and tolerance varies across different people is partially influenced by how they are experiencing the moment-to-moment user flow in your solution (be it a software application, a product, or a service). A simple interaction, say programming a DVR to record a TV show, can be "smooth" to one person who wants to record a TV show that is starting in an hour, but not so for another person who wants to record a TV show that is starting in a minute. All this translates into user satisfaction. Poor user flow makes users feel unproductive, ineffectual, anxious, and so forth. Optimal user flow makes users feel more productive, empowered, and creative.

We can arbitrarily define how smooth and enjoyable your solution is as the user flow, but within the context of human-computer interaction, user flow can mean several related things. The first possible definition is really just an overview of your solution that gives a sense of where users can navigate in your product. User flow can also mean the actual sequence of steps or path that the users take to accomplish a specific given task. The third possible definition is the actual quality and experience of the path they took to accomplish a task. Let's take a closer look at all three.

User Flow as a Map

A flowchart (or some other type of diagram) can sometimes be useful in giving an overview of the possible routes that users can take when they are using your solution. This form of visual aid can be described as the user flow map. Such visualization gives the designers, engineers, or architects a sense of the possible paths, scope, and complexity of the design of a system and can often help identify deficiencies, dependencies, or gaps in the architecture of your solution (see Figure 8.1). This should not be confused with a flow diagram that shows some work unit document or some data flow through the system as it is being processed. This other form of diagram commonly expresses the workflow, process flow, or data flow. Although this is more process-centric, a user flow map is person-centric. That is, instead of focusing on the process, user flow maps focus on the user. Common terms that are used to describe such user flow diagrams include *user interface flow, user navigation, task flow, interaction flow,* and *activity flow.*

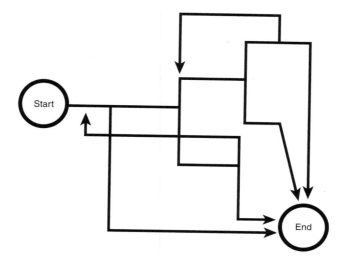

FIGURE 8.1

A user flow as a map gives an overview of the possible routes that users can take when they are using your solution.

User Flow as a Path

A user flow diagram such as the one in Figure 8.1 is relatively simple and may only be realistic in describing simple systems and solutions, such as an automated customer helpline or an ATM machine, where the user interaction is limited. More realistically, your solution will have more decision forks, processes, steps, and dependencies. In either case, sometimes you might have to demonstrate or test the user flow in a specific use case. Suppose you are designing a system that helps college students register for courses. Your system has to check whether there are any bursar's office holds, whether the course has any prerequisite, and other requirements. Let's further suppose that for 85% of the cases, there will be no issues with a student registering for a course. You might want to pick that specific scenario to show the user flow path in that scenario (see Figure 8.2). User flow, in this definition, describes the steps, milestones, and decisions made by the user along the way of a specific path. This is commonly used as early as the specification and design phase in the product cycle to define user experience, and as late as the testing phase. Similar usability techniques to capture user flow in this sense include cognitive walkthroughs, use cases, scenarios, usage scenarios, and storyboarding.

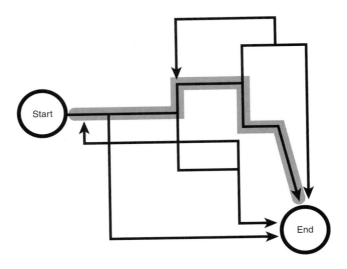

FIGURE 8.2

A user flow as a path describes the steps, milestones, and decisions made by the user along the way of a specific path in your solution.

User Flow as an Experience

A third way to define user flow, which is the focus of this chapter, is to focus on not the path but on the experience of the journey (see Figure 8.3). A good analogy is to relate the user flow path to a travel itinerary—it tells you the stops, the turns, the travel time, and so on—of a traveler. The experience of this journey, on the other hand, relates to the narrative of the traveler—the long check-ins, the crying baby on the flight, the terrible food, and so forth. To be clear, there is nothing wrong with documenting user flow paths to design or improve a system, to identify gaps, or to streamline processes. What paths do not capture are the quality of each interaction and what is going through the user's mind along the way. Whereas a user path focuses and outlines the entire journey from A to Z, a user flow focuses on the user and captures each moment-to-moment quality during the journey.

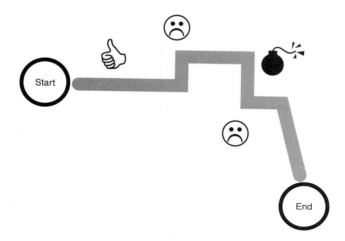

FIGURE 8.3

A user flow as an experience conveys the quality of a specific path.

Optimizing User Flow

The best place to start to understand and appreciate user flow is to introduce the work of Mihaly Csikszentmihalyi's on the psychology of flow. The psychology professor defines flow as a state where a person is

> being completely involved in an activity for its own sake. The ego falls away. Time flies. Every action, movement, and thought follows inevitably from the previous one, like playing jazz. Your whole being is involved, and you're using your skills to the utmost.

In the most simplistic terms, flow is like the Zen-like moment where you will find yourself engrossed in doing some activity. There are two important distinctions about flow and performance. First, flow is not about the speed at which a task is completed because perception of time is often distorted during a state of flow. Second, flow is not about accuracy or success rates; people who attained flow also frequently reported what Csikszentmihalyi calls an autotelic experience or "a self-contained activity, one that is done not with the expectation of some future benefit, but simply because the doing itself is the reward." That is, even if a task is not completed or is unsuccessful, the person still finds the experience enjoyable and rewarding.

A thorough explanation of the concept of flow is beyond the scope of this book, let alone this chapter, but for readers who are interested in this fascinating topic, Csikszentmihalyi's Flow: The Psychology of Optimal Experience is a must read. For now, suffice to say that Csikszentmihalyi has identified conditions in which flow is present. Some of these conditions are internal mental states, such as an autotelic experience or distorted time perception. Other conditions involve external factors, suggesting that they may be within the influence of the environment and other people. We can now take a look at three conditions of flow that have direct application to your solution.

1. Challenge-Skills Matching

In Csikszentmihalyi's model, flow is a state of optimal experience when there is a match between the challenge of a task and the person's skills. He explains that "enjoyment comes at a very specific point: whenever the opportunities for action perceived by the individual are equal to his or her capabilities." That is, when the perceived challenge of a task matches the person's skills, the person is said to be in what is called a *flow channel*. When the challenge of a task is higher than the skill of the person, the person will be in a state of anxiety because the task will be difficult. Conversely, when the skill of the person is higher than the challenge of the task, he or she will be bored because the task will be too easy (see Figure 8.4).

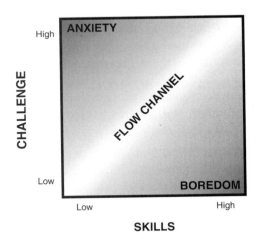

FIGURE 8.4

In Csikszentmihalyi's model, when the perceived challenge of a task matches the person's skills, the person is in the flow channel. When the challenge of a task is higher than the skill of the person, the person will be in a state of anxiety. When the skill of the person is higher than the challenge of the task, he or she will be bored because the task will be too easy.

An important factor to consider is the usage difficulty of your solution as perceived by your user. The important key here is that we are talking about the perceived challenge, not the actual complexity of the solution. For example, an ATM machine should rank low in usage difficulty for a person who uses it frequently, but high for a child who has never used one before. Likewise, CAD software can look intimidating to a person who has never used it before, thus ranking high in difficulty, but not so to an architect who uses it every day. A related point to remember is that perception of how difficult or challenging something is changes over time. With training, for example, the perceived difficulty can diminish. In the same token, without adequate training/experience, or with continued failures, perceived difficulty can increase.

WHAT CAN YOU DO?

Adjust challenges to match the skill level of your user. Some of your users may be new to using your solution, whereas others might have used an earlier version or have experience using a similar solution and will be able to leverage former knowledge. For example, in Figure 8.5, a novice user is hoping to rotate a picture, but unfortunately, the UI of the application is too complex for the user. Thus, the simple task has essentially become a challenging task. According to Csikszentmihalyi's model, this is where anxiety kicks in. One possible remedy in this case is to build in to the application a mechanism that can either adapt or be adjusted to an environment or mode that will match the user's skills. Many applications prompt users for their skill levels during installation or during the start of the application. Others allow users to toggle or switch between modes, such as between Basic and Advanced.

Csikszentmihalyi reports that at the height of the flow experience, people report a loss of self-consciousness and an altered sense of time, among other internal sensations. However, it is important to remember that not every user is expected to reach Zen-like states when using your solution. A bank customer doesn't need to feel self-consciousness while withdrawing money from an ATM. A package deliveryman will not likely need to experience a transcendent altered sense of time when entering shipping information into a handheld device. The important key here is to understand how perceived challenge relates to the user relevant skill level, and adjust the challenge accordingly.

In some cases, you might want to adjust the challenge to be lower than the skill level of the user. For example, if there is a reason to put users in an immediate comfort zone when using a new solution, you might want to make sure that their existing skill level can be leveraged to make them quickly proficient in the new solution: "If you know X, then Y will be a piece of cake!" A second instance when user skill levels should be higher than the challenge is when there is a high cost associated with making errors. In some mission-critical situations, errors made in a small task can delay or prevent the overall success of a project. Think medical equipment or sophisticated weapon systems. In these cases, you want the users and operators to be so well trained that interacting with the solution is second nature. There are also cases when the reverse—setting the challenge to be higher than the skill level—proves useful, such as in learning or training situations when it is ideal for the task to be just a little difficult for the user. Another instance when the challenge should sometimes be a little higher than the skill is games. Simply put, a game that is too easy is boring, as shown in Csikszentmihalyi's model (see Figure 8.4).

FIGURE 8.5

A novice user is hoping just to rotate a picture, but unfortunately the UI of the application is too complex for the user. A simple task has essentially become a challenging task.

2. Goals and Feedback

Typically, before users begin interacting with your solution, they will have an overall goal in mind (such as "I want to crop an image") and mental steps or subgoals (such as "Copy the image from my USB thumb drive, save it on my desktop, and open it in Super Photo Editor. When it is opened, I will drag the mouse over the image to define the region I want to crop."). Users don't typically articulate these steps, however, or follow them like a recipe unless they are narrating through a demonstration or are following written directions. More likely, these are memorized steps that some people like to call muscle memory. These clear mental goals, in Csikszentmihalyi's model, are vital to achieving flow.

The next thing you can do is to ensure that the feedback in your UI is immediate and unambiguous. Delayed feedback causes people to question whether they are attaining their goals or subgoals, and ambiguous feedback literally brings interaction to a halt and drains attention and focus as users attempt to understand the feedback to decide how to proceed (see Figure 8.6).

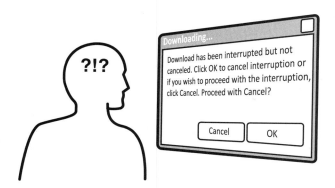

FIGURE 8.6

Ambiguous feedback literally brings interaction to a halt and drains attention and focus as users attempt to understand the feedback to decide how to proceed.

Make sure that UI feedback and all communication to the user is not ambiguous.
If you hear your user mumble something like, "Hmm, what does this do?" you may have an ambiguous UI that needs to be fixed. A good start is to think of your solution as a house with many rooms. You want to make sure that the doors are adequately loaded with symbols, text, or hints to where they lead. This is frequently referred to as *affordance* in the usability literature. These "doors" include tabs, buttons, and any other control that brings the user to the next step. A little redundancy here doesn't hurt. Even if the user misinterprets where the door leads to and "flows" into the wrong room, he or she can step out graciously and try alternative routes. The goal here is to keep users moving.

Learning through error is not an uncommon way for users interact with a new environment. Books have been written on how people learn through failure, and we have all heard of trial and error. Another reasonable learning approach is what I like to call the SWAT team approach: Have a target in mind, go into the house, systematically scan each room to hunt for your target. It is common to see users in real life and in usability labs resort to hovering the mouse over the menu items of an application (typically from left to right) and quickly scanning the drop-down choices to find a feature or function they want. Instead of relying on recollection ("The rotate command should be located under Edit, Image"), this systematic searching behavior is relying on recognition ("No…not here…nope…nope…there it is!").

The second thing you can do to make the UI less ambiguous is to organize and possibly trim the information presented to the user. Eye tracking will show that seasoned and savvy users typically do not spend much time reading the text in a dialog such as the one in Figure 8.6, especially if the paragraph looks too "chunky," such as more than three to four sentences. This behavior is likely due to the fact that the user has a preconceived idea about what is going on, and to maintain flow, the user chooses to proceed with what appears most logical.

Therefore, one approach and remedy is to presume that users will not read the majority of the text, and use verbs in the buttons that suggest the action that will be performed, instead of using the typical OK or Cancel labels (see Figure 8.7). If some paragraph of text must be included in the dialog, one technique is to include an unambiguous question at the end and place it in a separate line. Using the lower end of the continuous responsiveness class mentioned in Chapter 4, "Responsiveness," two seconds, and borrowing from known average reading speeds of adult English readers (about five words per second), use fewer than ten words, if possible, to maintain continuity.

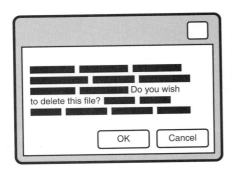 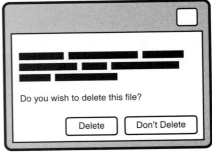

FIGURE 8.7

Eye-tracking studies show that some users avoid reading the text in dialogs when the paragraph appears too "chunky" (left). Two remedies are to use verbs in the buttons that suggest the action and to isolate the question at the end on a separate line.

3. Sense of Control

Not only may your users already have a sequence of steps in mind before they start engaging your solution, they may also have a set of alternative sequences to try if the primary one fails. Even if the users do not have to resort to alternative sequences, knowing at the back of their minds that there is more than one option is a critical factor in helping them stay in a state of flow. Csikszentmihalyi explains that "what people enjoy is not the sense of *being* in control, but the sense of *exercising* control in difficult situations." This is not different from how seasoned chess players keep in mind several alternative and consecutive moves in advance. The average chess master knows four to five moves in advance. (This is well studied and is called variation calculation.) As you can imagine, the feeling of having your only option fail is quite nerve-racking. The thought of having one of many options not working out, on the other hand, is quite tolerable: "If the network connection is down, I can still copy the spreadsheet onto a ZIP disk and hand it to Jennifer. If she doesn't have a Zip drive, I can put the file on my USB stick or burn the file onto a blank CD."

WHAT CAN YOU DO?

Provide undo features, escape hatches, back buttons, and so on. An important note about flow is that it is subjective and psychological. Just as you can't force or make someone have a pleasant journey, you don't exactly engineer flow in your solution. After all, it is a state of being experienced by your user. What you can do, however, is to make adjustments and modification in your solution to minimize or remove the obstacles that may block flow. An interaction without any visible means to bail out or backtrack is like creating a long stretch of highway that has no exits. Therefore, including undo options, escape hatches (cancel buttons, for example), and back buttons assures users that as they continue to move forward, they can move backward to correct a step; if they realize that they are on the wrong path, they can choose not to go forward. The objective then is not merely helping users make the right decisions all the time, but making it possible for them to correct wrong ones. Csikszentmihalyi writes that "the flow experience is typically described as involving a sense of control—or, more precisely, as lacking the sense of worry about losing control." Remember that the key here is to keep the users moving and, if the environment is new, encourage them to explore and learn.

Summary

Borrowing from Csikszentmihalyi's flow theory, this chapter discussed three ways by which you can ensure that user flow in your solution is optimal. The first concerns adjusting the challenge of using your solution to match the skill level of users. The second concerns providing clear goals and feedback by removing ambiguous communication in the UI. The last is to provide users with an environment in which they maintain their sense of potential control.

Rabbit Hole

Psychology of Flow

Csikszentmihalyi, M. (1975). *Beyond Boredom and Anxiety.* San Francisco: Jossey-Bass.

Csikszentmihalyi, M. (1990). *Flow: The Psychology of Optimal Experience.* New York: Harper & Row.

User Flow in HCI

Ghani, J. A. (1991). Flow in human-computer interactions: Test of a model. In J. Carey (Ed.), *Human Factors in Management Information Systems: An organizational perspective* (Vol. 3). Norwood, NJ: Ablex.

Ghani, J. A. and S. P. Desphande (1993). Task characteristics and the experience of optimal flow in human-computer interaction. *The Journal of Psychology,* 128, 381–391.

User Flow and Web Users

Pace, S. (2004). A grounded theory of the flow experiences of Web users. *International Journal of Human-Computer Studies,* 60, 327–363.

Pace, S. (2004). Designing for flow. Proceedings of AusWeb04, the Tenth Australian World Wide Web Conference, Southern Cross University, Lismore, 8–12.

Pace, S. (2000). Understanding the flow experiences of Web users. In *OZCHI 2000 Conference Companion: Interfacing Reality in the New Millennium,* (Eds.) C. Paris, N. Ozkan, S. Howard and S. Lu, CSIRO Mathematical and Information Sciences, North Ryde, Sydney, 2–5.

Pace, S. (2004). The roles of challenge and skill in the flow experiences of Web users. *Journal of Issues in Informing Science and Information Technology,* 1, 341–358.

Reading Speed

Fry, E. (1963). *Teaching Faster Reading: A manual.* Cambridge: Cambridge University Press.

Ziefle, M. (1998). Effects of display resolution on visual performance. *Human Factors,* 40, 555–568. (Author's note: Reading speed on monitors is ~10% slower than reading speed on printed material.)

9

Testing Time

In some situations, you need to collect timing data. Sometimes this results from a need to compare against benchmarks or to verify that performance objectives have been met. These are measurements taken against the system. Other times, you need to take measurements against the people who use your system. This might result from users' feedback of poor performance in your system. In either case, collecting reliable and valid data is critical. This chapter talks about various approaches to collecting data for actual duration, perceived duration, and user tolerance.

Putting Time to the Test

When users complain that your product or some feature of your product is slow, you might have to put on the research hat and get some data to verify whether the complaint is valid, and if so, what you can or cannot do about it. Other times, users may report that your product is slower than a competitor's. In this case, it would be wise to collect the numbers to determine whether there is indeed a real and significant difference between the two. Things get interesting when there is no difference but users are still reporting that your product is inferior. In this case, you might be dealing with a perception or tolerance issue (see Figure 9.1). In the following section, we discuss when and how you can go about clocking actual durations, measuring perceived duration, and assessing user tolerance.

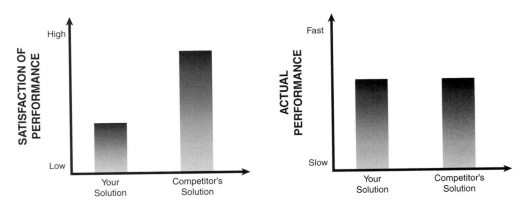

FIGURE 9.1

A comparison might confirm that users indeed rate your competitor's solution better in terms of performance, responsiveness, and so on (left). However, a comparison of the actual performance of the two (right) might reveal that, objectively, actual performance of the two may have no difference at all. In this case, you might be dealing with a perception or tolerance issue.

Collecting Reliable and Valid Data

Students in experimental design courses cannot escape two words—*reliability* and *validity*—when it comes to collecting data. Reliability, as the name suggests, concerns how reliable your data is. That is, if you were to collect the data in the same way you did the first time, would you get the same data again? If not, your data is not reliable. Validity concerns whether the data you collected is indeed reflecting or representing what you were trying to collect. That is, are you really measuring what you are trying to measure? Some experimentation can sometimes help verify the validity of your data. For example, suppose you are interested in measuring download duration for 10MB of data. You can artificially half and double the size of the data to be downloaded and see whether the download durations change systematically as expected. Although this cannot prove that your data is 100% valid, it can tell you whether it is not. For example, if the download durations stay the same, your data might not be valid. In this instance, you might be measuring something else (see Figure 9.2).

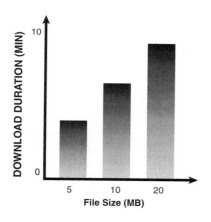 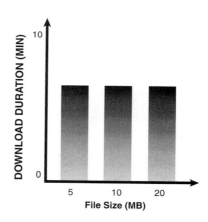

FIGURE 9.2

The data on the left chart shows a possible and expected pattern as the file size increases. However, if the download durations stay the same (right) despite increasing or decreasing the file size, the way by which you are measuring download duration might not be valid. In this instance, you might be measuring something else!

Because validity and reliability are independent of each other, it is possible to end up with one of four possible sets of data (see Figure 9.3) that are (1) reliable but not valid, (2) not reliable but valid, (3) not reliable and not valid, and finally, what you should aim for, (4) reliable and valid. It pays to spend some time to think about the reliability and validity of your data because decisions are usually made based on what the data suggests.

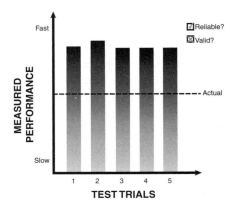
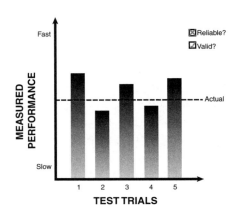
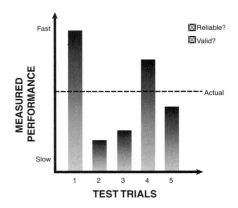
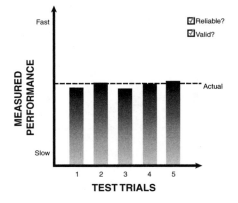

FIGURE 9.3

Because reliability and validity are independent, it is possible to end up with one of four possible sets of data: reliable but not valid (top left), not reliable but valid (top right), not reliable and not valid (bottom left), and finally, what you should aim for, reliable and valid (bottom right).

Clocking Actual Durations

When users report that your product or a particular feature of your product is slow, your immediate response should be to gather all the relevant facts to address the issue. One of the facts that is critical is the actual duration of the process in question. For a user who is complaining that it takes too long to log in to a system, this may be the duration between the user clicking a Log In button and the moment the user knows that he or she has successfully logged in. For a user who is browsing digital photographs, this might be the time it takes for the user to see the next picture after clicking a button with an arrow symbol (see Figure 9.4). Having objective durations is obviously the starting point in diagnosing many performance problems, but it is also the key to determining whether a reported issue is really a perception or tolerance issue. Although it is beyond the scope of this book to talk about the methods to collect actual durations, it is necessary to touch on a few pointers when it comes to clocking actual durations.

Define Actual Duration Carefully

An important point is how you define the start and end times of the process in question. Frequently, in software development, system response time is defined as the time it takes to complete the execution of a set of code or for a system to execute a command. However, if the interaction is initiated by the user—say, by a mouse-click, key press, or voice command—the start time ought to be set at the moment the user provides the command, and the end time should be set at the moment users perceive that the desired or intended command has been completely executed.

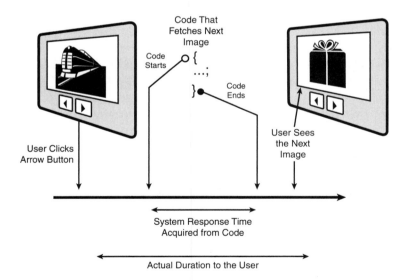

FIGURE 9.4

The system response time in this example is typically defined as the time it takes to execute the set of code to retrieve the next picture. However, to the user, the actual duration begins with the moment the user clicks the button to the time the user sees the next image on the screen.

For example, research has shown that it can take from around 10 to more than 70 milliseconds for a key press to be detected by the operating system, and depending on the refresh rate of the monitor, some more time to paint the screen. Therefore, as a rule of thumb, add 50 milliseconds to response times obtained through code when system response time is defined as the moment users provide an input (for example, a mouse click) to the moment the user perceives that the input has been received by the system (button depressing). If system response time is evaluated strictly from a system performance perspective, adding the extra 50 milliseconds is not necessary.

Choose the Right Precision

Different interaction requires different precision. One quick way to determine what precision you need is to ask yourself whether a 0.001-second difference is meaningful to you and the user. If it is, you need millisecond precision. If not, move up the scale to 0.01 seconds and ask whether that difference would be meaningful to you and your user. Keep increasing the magnitude until you reach a point where you know the difference would matter. For example, if a particular feature in your product takes between 5 and 10 seconds to complete, a 0.001-second, 0.01-second, and 0.1-second difference will not be meaningful. However, a one-second difference, say between five and six seconds, might begin to matter. Therefore, you will draw the line here and require a precision to the second for your data.

A difference of a few milliseconds is typically imperceptible to the user (0.321 seconds versus 0.322 seconds, for instance) unless and until multiple differences add up to a point where users begin to notice. In a previous chapter, we talked about the 20% Rule and how there is a better chance for users to detect a difference when one duration is 20% more or less than another duration. However, humans have physiological limitations that cap our ability to detect very small timing differences. For example, we cannot detect a difference of one millisecond. Research suggests that the minimum threshold for time detection is around 15 milliseconds. Human detection of music pitch, as a related example, happens only beyond 20 milliseconds. Beneath this threshold, everything sounds more like a click.

As far as the users and UI are concerned, interactions that are expected to be instantaneous will typically require precision in the tenths to hundredths of a second. Direct user input, such as key presses, mouse movements, mouse clicks, sketching, and touch screens, will typically require such precision. Longer interactions, such as installing a software application, will not likely need the same level of precision. Figure 9.5 shows some required precision and data-collection methods for some typical types of user interaction.

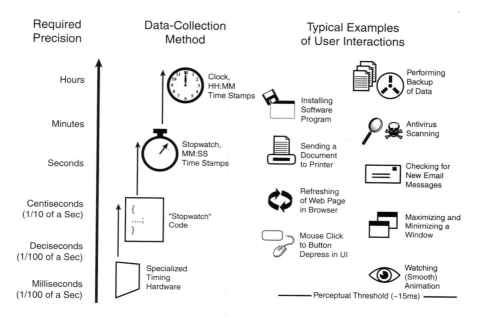

FIGURE 9.5

Required precision and data-collection methods for some typical types of user interaction. Direct user input, such as key presses, mouse movements, mouse clicks, sketching, and touch screens, will typically require decisecond precision. Longer interactions, such as installing a software application, will not likely need the same level of precision.

Choose the Right Method

Depending on the precision required, there are a few ways to collect timing data. For measurements that require very high precision, you might have to consider the use of specialized equipment, such as Measurement Computing's PCI-CTR05. These specialized timers and counters typically have their own clocks that are independent of the computer system clock and are frequently installed in a separate system altogether. For mainstream applications, such an approach is typically overkill. More commonly and more easily, timing data can be collected via software using code for interactions and processes that require fairly precise measurement. Table 9.1 shows some examples of stopwatch codes. Using actual stopwatches and MM:SS time stamps are acceptable only when second-level precision is acceptable, such as for downloads that last for several seconds and beyond.

Table 9.1 Simple Examples of Obtaining Actual Duration in Code in Various Programming Languages

Programming Language	"Stopwatch" Code

Visual Basic	```Dim sw As New Stopwatch```
	```sw.Start()```
	```'Perform something here```
	```sw.Stop()```
	```Console.WriteLine(sw.ElapsedMilliseconds)```
	```Console.ReadLine()```

C#	```Stopwatch sw = new Stopwatch();```
	```sw.Start();```
	```//Perform something here```
	```sw.Stop();```
	```Console.WriteLine(sw.ElapsedMilliseconds);```
	```Console.ReadLine();```

C++	```Stopwatch^ sw = gcnew Stopwatch;```
	```Sw->Start();```
	```//Perform something here```
	```Sw->Stop();```
	```Console::WriteLine(sw->ElapsedMilliseconds);```
	```Console::ReadLine();```

ActionScript (Adobe)	```var stopwatch:Stopwatch = new Stopwatch();```
	```stopwatch.start();```
	```//Perform something here```
	```trace(Stopwatch.stop());```

Java	```long startTime = System.currentTimeMillis();```
	```//Perform something here```
	```long stopTime = System.currentTimeMillis();```
	```System.out.println(stopTime — startTime);```

PHP	```$stimer = explode(' ', microtime());```
	```$stimer = $stimer[1] + $stimer[0];```
	```//Perform something here```
	```$etimer = explode(' ', microtime());```
	```$etimer = $etimer[1] + $etimer[0];```
	```printf($etimer-$stimer));```

Note that overhead in user input and result display must be factored into the timing reported by such methods.

Do Not Use Your Users as Clocks!

When people are prepared to time duration, the tendency is to use some mental or sub-vocal counting techniques ("one-one thousand, two-one thousand…"). More often, people recall from memory how long some event lasted. In this instance, most people are prone to gravitating toward time anchors ("about five minutes," "less than three seconds," and so on) in reporting how long some event lasted. Although the former is probably more accurate than the latter, both are inadequate measures of objective time. Therefore, durations reported by users should be regarded as only estimates at best. Objective time must be measured by objective means!

Measuring Perceived Duration

Measuring perceived duration is not as straightforward as clocking actual duration, but sometimes you will need to measure perceived duration as you would measure actual duration. The following sections introduce some possible techniques to measure perceived duration. Remember that the objective here is to get some numeric value that can be compared against actual duration, not to assess satisfaction or perception of speed.

Verbal Estimation

The simplest approach to getting perceived duration is just to have users tell you how long some event was. The limitation of verbal estimation is that people are susceptible to reporting their estimations in time anchors. One possible remedy to counter the anchoring effect is to improvise a way to have users provide their estimation on a scale. For example, after having users interact with a particular feature, you can ask users to state a lower limit and an upper limit of the duration of the feature. That is, "X was more than 5 seconds, but no more than 15 seconds." Set these lower and upper limits on opposite ends of a scale, with no numbers or tick marks in between, and have users place a point between the two extremes to indicate how long X felt like relative to those two extremes. A numeric value can then be calculated with a little high school math. Figure 9.6 illustrates these steps.

Step 1. Have user interacts with feature.

Step 2. Ask user to state a minimum and maximum limit of the duration.

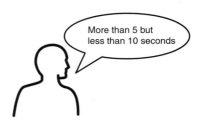

More than 5 but less than 10 seconds

Step 3. Create a scale with the two limits with no marks in between.

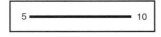

5 ——————— 10

Step 4. Have users indicate a point between the two limits to show how long the duration was.

Step 5. Calculate the value relative to the two limits.

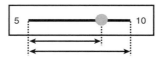

5 ——————— 10

FIGURE 9.6

The limitation of verbal estimation is that people are susceptible to reporting their estimations in time anchors. This diagram illustrates one technique to counter the anchoring effect.

Reproduction

Another technique that can be considered to obtain perceived duration from users is to have them re-create the event by narrating, or use a stopwatch, or simulate the event to show when it started and ended. You will be timing how long the re-creation or reproduction lasted and using that timing as the perceived duration. For example, suppose the task is for a user to click a button to start a search. When the results appear on a data grid, the interaction is deemed complete. After the interaction, give users a stopwatch and have them start and stop the stopwatch to indicate how long they think the search took. Alternatively, give them some means to digitally re-create their interaction. In either case, with several trials, this can give you a fairly good estimate of perceived time. The limitation in this approach is that this works well with relatively shorter durations.

Adjustment

A related technique to reproduction is to allow users to adjust the speed of an event (such as a video playback) until the speed matches what he or she believes was the duration of the event. For example, suppose users go to a website and watch a sequence of events as the Web page fully loads. Have the users view a video sequence of the loading of the Web page and make it possible for them to adjust the playback speed until it matches what they believe was the actual speed, making sure that the users don't see any value or indication of the amount of each adjustment. In addition, for as many trials as you can run with the user, you want to start the speed of the playback at a random speed. So, if the playback starts off slow, users will increase its speed, and vice versa. As in any other technique, several trial runs are better than just one. For this technique, it is not uncommon to see data clustering above and below the actual duration. One cluster will likely represent the trials when users increased the speed, and the other when users decreased the speed (see Figure 9.7). Without going into detail, this is likely the result of the user's perceptual detection threshold. Remember the 20% Rule?

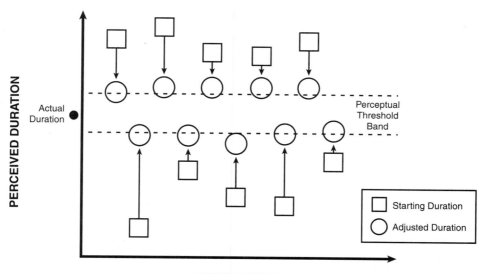

FIGURE 9.7

For the adjustment technique, it is not uncommon to see two clusters of data points, one from trials when users increased the speed and one from when users decreased the speed.

Assessing Tolerance

In a previous chapter, we talked about how perceived duration is meaningless without taking tolerance into consideration. Having a user tell you that it takes ten seconds to pull up the client records from a database is not useful or meaningful by itself. However, when users add that it normally takes only two seconds, we begin to appreciate the situation better. There are various possible ways to assess tolerance, and this section describes some of them.

Responsiveness Expectation

The quickest and "cheapest" way to assess user tolerance is just to simply ask them. Instead of asking "How fast was X?" we ask "How fast should X be?" or "How fast is X normally?" Although this is one of the easiest and most direct means to assess tolerance, without pairing this with some other techniques, the data you get back might not prove very useful. One possible approach is to have users relate the responsiveness of an interaction to be evaluated against another interactions that the user is familiar with: "X should load as fast as Y" or "X should appear as faster than Y, but slower than Z."

Experimentation

Another easy way to assess tolerance is to systematically show users various prototypes or versions of the solution and just have them interact and rate each prototype on some scale of responsiveness. Ideally, you want to randomize the order by which the prototypes are tried and make sure that each prototype is shown more than once (see Figure 9.8). You can get creative with this technique if there is a reason to believe that some other factor is influencing people's tolerance. For example, you can create a series of prototypes, all of which have equal performance and responsiveness, but change branding, size of text, sound of the mouse clicks, and so on. This is not an uncommon technique in market/scientific research. Recently, for example, researchers found that kids preferred food wrapped in McDonald's wrappers than the same food wrapped in unmarked wrappers!

Step 1. Create various shells or skins of the same prototype.

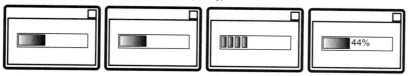

Step 2. Randomize the order of the prototypes for each user and have them interact with each more than once.

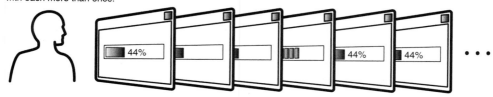

Step 3. For each prototype, have users give a rating of performance.

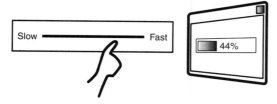

FIGURE 9.8

An easy way to assess tolerance is to systematically show users various prototypes or versions of the solution and just have them interact and rate each prototype on some scale of responsiveness.

Production

This technique is related to the reproduction technique discussed earlier. The idea is to have users simulate or narrate an interaction to get a sense of how responsive they expect the interaction to be. This is different from reproduction, where the user attempts to re-create what was experienced. In production, you simply tell the user to be the director and dictate how responsive the interaction should be.

Cross-Modality Matching

Another technique is called cross-modality matching. In this technique, you ask users to indicate the property of one dimension to indicate the magnitude of another. This is effective when the original property is difficult for the users to describe or express, or when you don't want the property of the original dimension distracting or influencing their estimation. Pediatricians often use a similar technique to help children express how much pain they are experiencing, by showing them a row of cartoon faces that express increasing levels of pain from one end to the other and having them point to a face that represents how much pain they are in (Figure 9.9). Although this technique is not susceptible to inaccurate verbal estimation, what you get from the user is a ratio, not a numeric value. Therefore, a good time to use this is when users have to compare the difference between two durations. The data you get will give you an idea of the magnitude of the difference perceived by the user between two durations.

FIGURE 9.9

Pediatricians often help children express how much pain they are experiencing by showing them a row of cartoon faces that express increasing levels of pain from one end to the other and having them point to a face that represents how much pain they are in.

Experimental Design Considerations

As mentioned, when people are prepared to time an event, they are very likely to use some mental technique to time it. In the context of human-computer interaction, this is problematic from a research perspective because most users do not consciously time every single interaction. More commonly, users rely on their memory and estimate the duration of some event: "It took over half an hour to install the program" or "The search took between five and ten minutes." The following are pointers to keep in mind to make sure that you are getting reliable and valid data.

Order Effects: Which Came First?

It is not uncommon to compare the duration between two products or solutions. There are pros and cons in having the same individual evaluate both solutions. One of the pros is that you will have pairs of data points that can be reliably put side by side for comparison because they came from the same person. This approach is called *within-subject* in experimental design. In a within-subject design, the user gets to interact with all the prototypes. In a *between-subject* design, each user gets to try only one type of prototype (see Figure 9.10). One of the biggest risks in the within-subject design is called order effects, which is essentially a situation where the order or sequence by which a person experiences two or more things actually influences his or her evaluation, judgment, or perception. Supposedly, as some have argued, the famous Coke-versus-Pepsi test, which resulted in Pepsi tasting better, was a result of order effect!

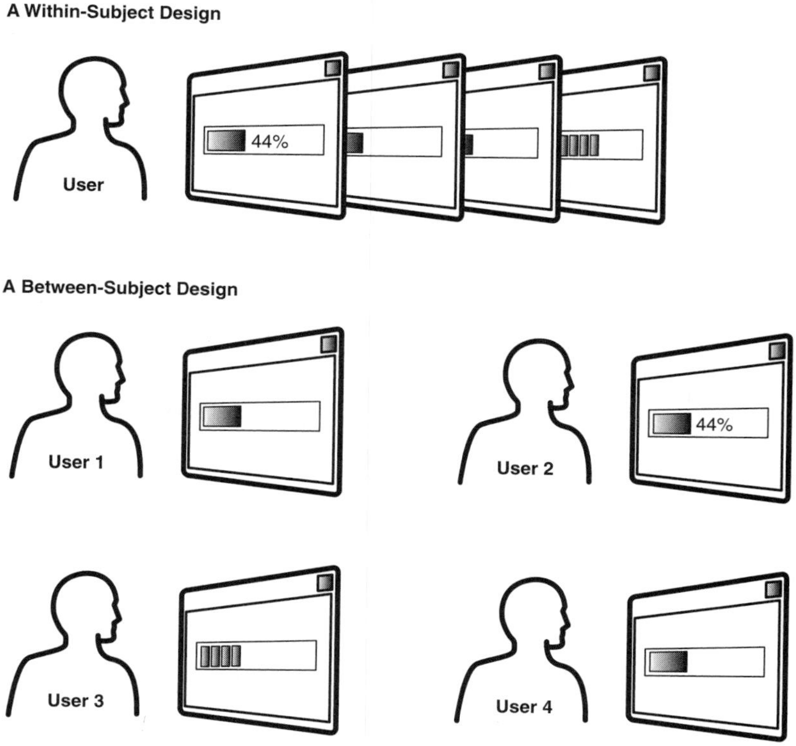

A Within-Subject Design

A Between-Subject Design

FIGURE 9.10

In a within-subject design, the user gets to interact with all the prototypes. In a between-subject design, each user gets to try only one type of prototype.

Exposure and Practice Effects

An ideal setup, if possible, is to have users experience a longer sequence than just simply A-B. That is, have users go through an A-B-A-B-A-B sequence, for example. Time perception is susceptible to exposure and practice, so having a longer sequence allows for perception to "level off," theoretically giving you cleaner and more representative data. Remember the lesson of the Barnabus Effect: First exposure will seem longer than subsequent exposures.

Keep the Cat in the Bag!

As mentioned previously, people use different strategies to measure time. When they are prepared, they are likely to use mental techniques. When they have to look back in time, they will rely on memory. That said, once your users know that you are collecting time estimation data, they will not be able to resist timing their interaction with some mental counting. In many cases, we don't want that. Therefore, you do not want to tell the user (at least not until the end of your experiment) that you are interested in having them estimate the duration. Second, you want to make your goal of collecting time estimates inconspicuous to the user. One way to "disguise" your hypothesis is to sandwich the cue to estimate time in a series of questions. To further prevent users from guessing correctly that you are out to measure their time perception, you can even add in "dummy" trials that skip the question on time perception (see Figure 9.11).

Present the prototypes to the user.

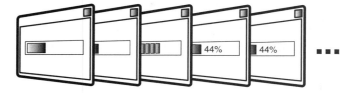

For each prototype, have users give a rating of various qualities and properties of each prototype. Sandwich the responsiveness question in the middle.

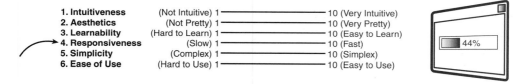

1. **Intuitiveness**	(Not Intuitive) 1 ———————— 10 (Very Intuitive)	
2. **Aesthetics**	(Not Pretty) 1 ———————— 10 (Very Pretty)	
3. **Learnability**	(Hard to Learn) 1 ———————— 10 (Easy to Learn)	
4. **Responsiveness**	(Slow) 1 ———————— 10 (Fast)	
5. **Simplicity**	(Complex) 1 ———————— 10 (Simplex)	
6. **Ease of Use**	(Hard to Use) 1 ———————— 10 (Easy to Use)	

To further prevent users from realizing that you are measuring time perception, remove the responsiveness question from a few trials.

| Trial 1 | Trial 2 | Trial 3 | Trial 4 | Trial 5 |

FIGURE 9.11

One way to "disguise" your hypothesis is to sandwich the cue to estimate time in a series of questions and remove the actual question of interest (responsiveness) from some of the trials.

Summary

Collecting reliable and valid data is critical in helping you diagnose real or perceived performance problems. In clocking actual durations, you have to define your actual duration carefully by considering what your user regards as the start and stop times that define a response time. Choosing the right precision and choosing the appropriate method to collect data will also be critical in securing reliable and valid data. To measure perceived time, you can have users report how long something felt, have them reproduce the duration, or have them adjust the duration to match what they remember. To assess tolerance, you can simply have users tell you what level of responsiveness they expect, show them and have them rate a series of some prototypes, let them simulate or narrate to convey their expectations, or have them rate the responsiveness on a scale not related to responsiveness. When collecting data on perceived duration and tolerance, it is good to keep certain snags in mind, such as order effects and practice effects. And finally, it is wise to prevent the user from guessing that you are measuring time perception by hiding your hypothesis.

Rabbit Hole

Testing Methodologies

Bindra, D. and H. Waksberg (1956). Methods and terminology in studies of time estimation. *Psychological Bulletin*, 53, 155–159.

Fraisse, P. (1984). Perception and estimation of time. *Annual Reviews of Psychology*, 35, 1–36.

Gescheider, G. A. (1977). *Psychophysics: Method and Theory*. NY: John Wiley and Sons.

Gescheider, G. A. (1985). *Psychophysics: Method, Theory, and Application*. Hillsdale, NJ: Lawrence Erlbaum Associates.

Zakay, D. (1993). Time estimation methods—do they influence prospective duration estimates? *Perception*, 22, 91–101.

Human Estimations of Time

Getty, D. (1976). Counting processes in human timing. *Perception & Psychophysics*, 20, 191–197.

Killeen, P. R. and N. A. Weiss (1987). Optimal timing and the Weber function. *Psychological Review*, 94, 455–468.

Yarmey, A. D. (2000). Retrospective duration estimations for variant and invariant events in field situations. *Applied Cognitive Psychology*, 14, 45–57.

Instrument Limitations

Beringer, J. (1992). Timing accuracy of mouse response registration on the IBM microcomputer family. *Behavior Research Methods, Instruments, & Computers,* 24, 486–490.

Shimizu, H. (2002). Measuring keyboard response delays by comparing keyboard and joystick inputs. *Behavior Research Methods, Instruments, & Computers,* 34, 250–256.

Ulrich, R. (1989). Time resolution of clocks: Effects on reaction time measurement: Good news for bad clocks. *British Journal of Mathematical and Statistical Psychology,* 42, 1–12.

10

Techniques

The techniques in this chapter fall into one of two general approaches that must be considered to improve the user experience of your product in terms of time and timing. The first approach is to make users feel that the actual duration of a process is shorter than it really is. This is called *perception management*. The second approach is to make users more tolerant of the duration. This approach is called *tolerance management*. This chapter describes both of these approaches that can be considered in the design of user interface (UI).

Perception Management

Generally, anything you can do to make users feel that the actual time taken to complete a process is shorter than it really is desirable. As mentioned in Chaper 4, "Responsiveness," it is possible to make something go too fast, but by and large, making users feel that time "flew" is desirable. In the following pages, we consider the following techniques that may be applied to your solution to make time "fly":

- Preemptive start
- Early completion
- Invisible deconstruction
- Descending durations
- Nonlinear progress indication
- Continuous durations
- Information
- Meaningful diversion
- Fire-and-forget

Preemptive Start

Frequently, there is no need to wait for the user to provide all inputs before proceeding with a process. Whenever possible, start the process instead of waiting until all inputs are provided.

HOW AND WHY IT WORKS

People can define a duration only when there is a clear start time and a clear end time. When users finally get to a point where they explicitly start the process, this is what they will naturally and mentally assume as the start time. A great example of when to apply this technique is a lengthy software install (Figure 10.1). Many installations require users to provide information about the installation path, program settings, and other customizations. When all the information is provided, the installation begins. Although this is systematic, some user information might not be required to start other processes, such as copying the installation files to a temporary installation folder on the user's computer.

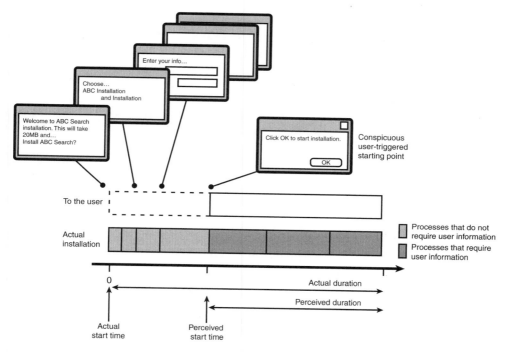

FIGURE 10.1

In the example above, while the user is filling out information for the installation of ABC Search, the installation program has already started. To the user, the perceived starting time of the installation is when the user explicitly starts the process when he or she clicks on the OK button.

KEEPING IN MIND

The processes that you kick off in this technique before users explicitly start the process should be processes that are "harmless" to the users and their environment. Consider legal, ethical, and other constraints when deciding which processes you can kick off preemptively. In addition, remember to build in mechanisms that will clean up any preemptive process if the user chooses not to proceed.

Early Completion

Just as you can preemptively start an event, you can prematurely "end" an event by either performing some processes in the background or delaying these processes to give users the impression that the entire process has completed. This works well with processes that have substantial cleanup work. Users can get anxious to start using your product or stop using it to move on to another task. So, instead of making users wait for your solution to finish cleaning up, allow them to start consuming your solution while it completes the processes that users do not need to see or care about it.

HOW AND WHY IT WORKS

Like the previous technique, this works because the end time is defined without the cleanup processes. In addition, this technique works because it is also "considerate" to the anxious user. Imagine if a Broadway play made its audience stay behind to watch the stage crew dismantle the props and clean up the stage!

KEEPING IN MIND

In Case A in Figure 10.2 when the installation is perceived to be complete, users may start to use the installed application immediately. If the cleanup process requires substantial processing power, this might result in a noticeable performance hit in the immediate use of the application. You might resolve this by delaying the cleanup (Case B) or limiting the amount of resources it can consume perhaps by spreading and thus "thinning" the cleanup process in the background.

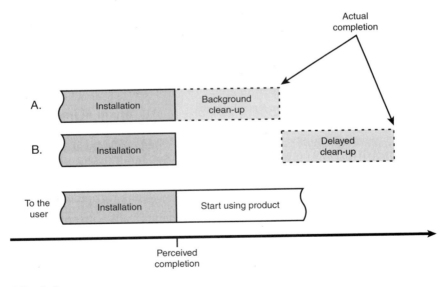

FIGURE 10.2

You can prematurely "end" an event by either performing some processes in the background (Case A) or delaying these processes (Case B) to give users the impression that the entire process has completed. This allows users to consume or use your product immediately.

Invisible Deconstruction

Related to the preceding technique, this technique calls for you to unload and deconstruct components of your solution that users do not need to see. For example, in the closing of an application, as shown in Figure 10.3, there is little need for users to see the sequence of parts of your application disappearing. Instead, as soon as users close the application, the entire UI should disappear immediately, and any necessary unloading and deconstruction can happen invisibly in the background.

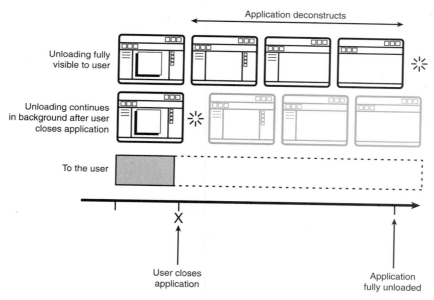

FIGURE 10.3

As soon as users close the application, the entire UI should disappear immediately, and any necessary unloading and deconstruction can happen invisibly in the background.

HOW AND WHY IT WORKS

This technique works for the same reasons that make early completion work. This is essentially an "out of sight, out of mind" principle. The technique further gives the illusion of responsiveness when it appears to close on the user's command. Because people use changes in the environment to tell time, from a psychological perspective, this technique makes the changes invisible to the user, making it not possible for users to tell how much time was taken to unload the UI.

KEEPING IN MIND

Because this technique works like the Early completion technique, you will have to consider any overhead in the deconstruction process itself. If the deconstruction requires substantial processing power, it may be wise to "thin-out" the process in the background so that it doesn't cause too much performance degradation.

Descending Durations

Many lengthy processes are made up of multiple discrete subprocesses that are meaningful to the user (Figure 10.4). An installation of an application, for example, may require the installation of supporting engines, technologies, or some other prerequisites. Whenever possible, arrange the order of the subprocesses such that the subprocess with the longest duration starts first.

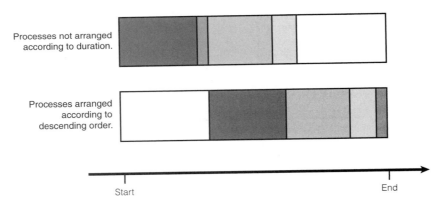

Processes not arranged according to duration.

Processes arranged according to descending order.

Start   End

FIGURE 10.4

At the top, we have a process that is made up of five subprocesses that have various durations. For long running processes, rearrange the subprocesses such that the shortest running subprocess is at the end.

HOW AND WHY IT WORKS

Not many users like to watch an entire process when it is lengthy. The tendency for most, when it comes to time-consuming tasks, is to get an idea of how long the task will be, attend to another task, and return to the process when it is near completion. Because users are more likely to watch the tail end of the task, having the short-running subprocesses at the end is better because it is more encouraging to see rapid progress with short-running subprocesses than apparent slow progress with the long-running ones.

KEEPING IN MIND

This technique works well with long-running tasks because users will be more tolerant of short-running tasks and might be more likely to watch the entire process. For long-running tasks, always give users an idea of remaining time or remaining subprocesses because they likely attend to other tasks and return to check the progress of the installation sporadically.

Nonlinear Progress Indication

For long running processes, instead of reporting progress indication in a linear way (50% means exactly half done), you can report progress nonlinearly, as shown in Figure 10.5. In doing so, the progress seems rapid when users periodically check on its progress. This borrows from the descending durations technique, but instead of telling the users the remaining subprocesses to be completed, this technique reports an overall percentage or time remaining.

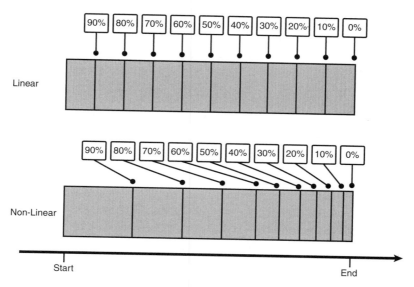

FIGURE 10.5

In the example above, because the progress is reported in a nonlinear fashion, the progress of the process seems more rapid when users witness the tail end of the process, as users commonly do for long-running processes.

HOW AND WHY IT WORKS

This technique works in the same way as the descending duration technique in that it takes advantage of the fact that people are more likely to view the tail end of long-running tasks. The logic behind not keeping progress linear for this technique is because not every 10% or ten-minute block is perceived equally. As users lose patience and tolerance with a long-running task, the same ten-minute block seems longer and longer each time.

KEEPING IN MIND

This technique assumes that having exact work or time remaining values is not critical to the user. That is, your users are not relying on the values to make critical decisions or to perform mission-critical tasks. Remember that it works best for long-running tasks and that users have to know that it is a long-running task. Giving users an idea of how long the process takes to complete is critical.

Continuous Durations

Ask for all user input up front, and have the task continue unattended all the way to completion instead of pausing midprocess to prompt users for more information. This situation occurs frequently in installation, but can also be found in other interactions. An example, as shown in Figure 10.6, is a photo-editing program that prompts users for several inputs to complete a task.

HOW AND WHY IT WORKS

Nothing is more frustrating than returning to a process that you thought you had started an hour ago only to discover the UI was actually waiting for you to click Confirm if you *really* wanted to proceed. Asking questions in a step-by-step approach, although systematic, creates multiple blocks of duration that not only cause time to be perceived as longer, but might cause actual time taken to complete the task to be longer, too.

KEEPING IN MIND

For applications such as photo editing, there might be an argument to walk users through each step so they know how the image is being manipulated at each step. A possible alternative is to walk them through each step, but instead of manipulating the actual file, show and manipulate a thumbnail of the actual image to allow users to preview how the image is manipulated.

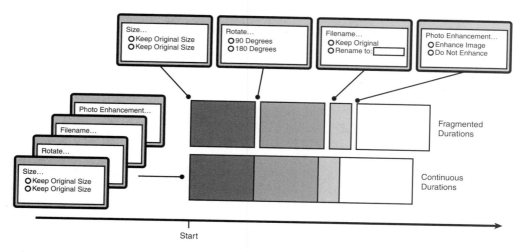

FIGURE 10.6

In this example, the application asks for all user input up front (bottom blocks), and the tasks continue all the way to completion unattended. This prevents midprocess interruptions that essentially create multiple blocks of duration that may be perceived to be longer than the actual time taken.

Information

Give users the right amount, level, and type of information on how long a process or task takes (Figure 10.7). Research has shown that bank customers who were given information about a wait perceive the wait to be shorter than its actual duration. As mentioned in Chapter 6, "Progress Indication," the amount, level, and type of information depends on what your users find meaningful and what they realistically do with the information.

HOW AND WHY IT WORKS

Uncertainty about how long something will last creates the biggest distortion of time. Giving users information about how long something takes or how much longer it will take gives them some level of certainty and comfort that things are progressing. In addition, it allows them to feel more efficient and productive because they can attend to other tasks while the process is ongoing.

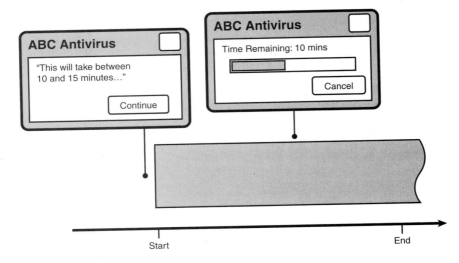

FIGURE 10.7

The two dialogs give users information about how long the antivirus program will run, but each uses a different amount, level, and type of information depending on the state of the process.

KEEPING IN MIND

Remember to use time anchors when expressing time estimates. Always ask whether the information is meaningful to and can be acted upon by the user. A database administrator probably needs to see more details of a backup in progress, whereas an office user probably doesn't need to see the mysterious system files that are being loaded as his e-mail program is starting up.

Meaningful Diversion

This technique borrows from the adage "Time flies when you are having fun." During a lengthy task or process, present information to the user that will be engaging or valuable to the user. This is often done in lengthy installations.

HOW AND WHY IT WORKS

This simple and widely practiced technique (think theme park) works not just because users are distracted from the wait. The distraction itself has to have some value to the user for users to "forget" that they are waiting for a process to complete. In addition, some relevance to the actual process is better than putting in a diversion unrelated to the process. In the example in Figure 10.8 where the user is installing a game, it makes sense to make learning about weapons in the game one of the options. The more you make the user interact with the diversion, the better. That is, making them click through a series of interactive slides is better than having them watch an automatic slide show.

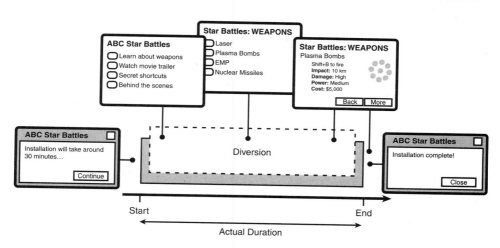

FIGURE 10.8

During a very lengthy task or process, present information to the user that is engaging or valuable to the user.

KEEPING IN MIND

With more diversion options (secret weapons shortcut, behind the scenes, etc.), you stand a higher chance of satisfying more users because everybody values things differently. One man's meat is another man's poison. That said, each diversion should be light-weight and not cause substantial overhead in the performance of the actual process itself. In addition, looping through the same content like a slide show is not good practice (and is identified as a violation in the next chapter).

Fire-and-Forget

Some processes and tasks, unlike installations or downloads, do not have any tangible value or purpose to users after they complete them. The value in these processes is that they complete successfully. Examples include system maintenance tasks, such as scheduled antivirus scanning. For such processes, inform users that the process completes in the background, as shown in the ABC backup example in Figure 10.9. Consider a notification of completion, too.

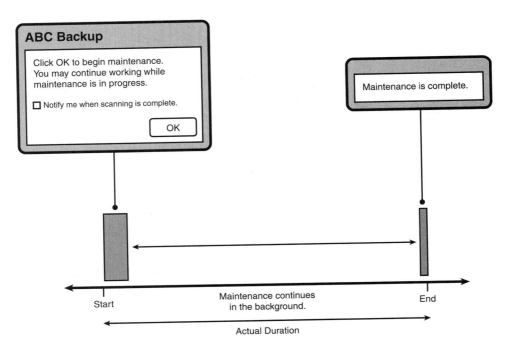

FIGURE 10.9

For processes that have little tangible value or purpose after completion, inform users that the process will complete in the background and consider a notification of completion.

HOW AND WHY IT WORKS

This technique borrows from the saying "out of sight, out of mind." Research has shown that under many circumstances, the perception of the duration between two points in time is longer when there is activity between the two points than when there is no activity. This is called the *filled-duration illusion*. That is, a ten-second beep is typically judged longer than two beeps spaced ten seconds apart.

KEEPING IN MIND

The critical factor in making this technique effective is distraction: Ensure that users are discouraged from waiting for the process to complete. If users wait out the process, the wait is not exactly "out of mind" and will likely produce the opposite effect. This is what some research has shown: Unfilled or unoccupied time feels longer than filled or occupied time. Absence will make the heart grow fonder! There are some simple ways to distract them from the absence—for example, by encouraging them to continue with their work, or offering to automatically perform a task when the process completes (such as shutting down the computer). In addition, it is important to enable users to check on the progress and stop the process if they need to (to shut down the computer, for example).

Tolerance Management

In many instances, it is impossible to make users believe that actual time is shorter than it really is. Generally, these are during longer durations, such as when installing software or antivirus scanning. In such instances, consider using (or complementing perception management with) tolerance management. These tolerance management techniques do not attempt to disguise a lengthy process, but instead aim to make users more tolerant and patient. In the following pages, we consider eight of these techniques.

- Underpromise, overdeliver
- The Priceline model
- Time anchors
- Worth the wait
- Buffer and offer
- First-time, one-time only
- Contextualized benchmarks
- End on time

Underpromise, Overdeliver

When stating how much time a process will take, estimate slightly longer than the actual duration. When the process finishes earlier than the stated estimate, the early completion is welcomed as a "bonus."

HOW AND WHY IT WORKS

Many businesses and service industries use this technique. In restaurants, many hosts and hostesses tell diners that their wait will be longer than they really anticipate it will be. When diners get their table earlier than expected, they are pleasantly surprised. This is the same technique employed by theme parks, such as Walt Disney World and Disneyland, where the displayed estimated wait times for rides are typically longer than average actual wait times.

KEEPING IN MIND

Do not go overboard when overstating the estimated duration. That is, if the process reliably finishes in eight minutes (see Figure 10.10), you do not want to say that it will be completed in 30 minutes. A rule of thumb is to use the next higher time anchor (as discussed in Chapter 7, "Expressing Time").

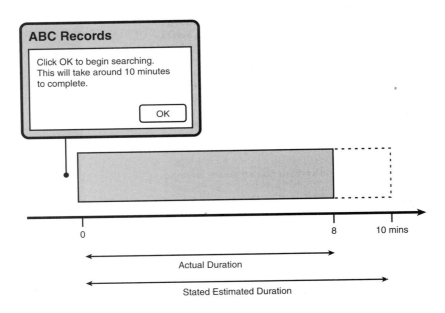

FIGURE 10.10

The example above states an estimated duration of 10 minutes although the actual duration is really 8 minutes. When the process completes before the stated time, the early completion is welcomed.

The Priceline Model

During a long-running task, communicate the value of the task to users. If users understand that the system is performing a task that benefits them or brings them value that they cannot get through other means, they will be more tolerant of the wait.

HOW AND WHY IT WORKS

This technique works by building user tolerance by assuring and reminding users of the value of the actual process. In the example in Figure 10.11, for example, the user is told that the antivirus program is performing an "aggressive" detection of his system. This "value" encourages the user to let the task complete in contrast to when the UI simply states "scanning." The name of this technique comes from airfare websites that promise users that they are searching through "millions of deals" to find them the best offer. If you want the best deals, you want them to do a thorough search, don't you?

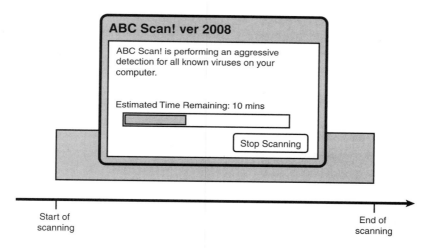

FIGURE 10.11

In this example, the antivirus program explicitly informs the user that it is performing a vital and important task that is valuable and beneficial to the user. This builds user tolerance since the user knows that the wait translates into some tangible value for him or her.

KEEPING IN MIND

The value that you communicate to users has to be valuable to them. A user who actually starts a scanning process will likely be aware of the value and purpose of the scanning process, and therefore be more tolerant of the duration. A scheduled scan that starts automatically without user intervention, on the other hand, might not be tolerated as well. In this case, some other value of scanning must be communicated to the user, such as "There have been 142 new known viruses since the last time your computer was scanned."

Time Anchors

Use time anchors to express time in the UI, particularly when stating maximum time ("less than"), estimated remaining time, estimated range, or frequency.

HOW AND WHY IT WORKS

Refer to page 104 in Chapter 7, "Expressing Time," for more on time anchors.

KEEPING IN MIND

Time anchors are useful for the system to express time to the users, but not necessarily vice versa. In the lower-right example in Figure 10.12, for example, clicking the Change button should provide users an option to specify any duration they want (1, 2, 3, 4, 5, 6, etc.) not just time anchors.

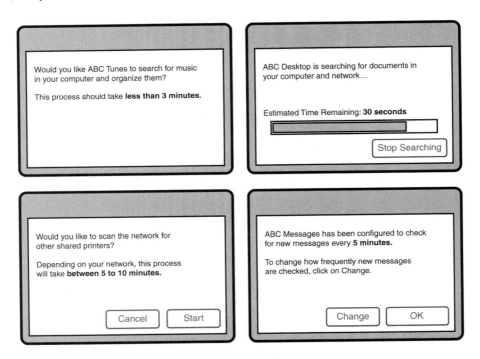

FIGURE 10.12

In the examples above, time anchors are used to express state maximum time (upper left), estimated time remaining (upper right), estimated range (lower left) and frequency (lower right).

Worth the Wait

Ensure users that the wait will be worth it and make sure that what users get at the end of a wait matches or surpasses what they expect. You want them to feel that it was "worth the wait." When users have to repeat the same process in the future, they will be more tolerant of the wait.

HOW AND WHY IT WORKS

The effectiveness of this technique hinges on building tolerance during the wait and securing satisfaction after the wait (Figure 10.13). Many restaurants, for example, proudly display rave reviews from magazines and newspapers in their waiting areas. Beyond fame and pride, these wall-mounted trophies work to build tolerance during a wait. Ensuring that service is indeed worth the wait is critical. Research has shown that a very positive value consumers receive at the end of a long wait can correct the negative perception that was formed during the long wait itself. That is, while standing in line, a consumer may first feel that the experience of waiting is absolutely terrible, but after receiving great service, the same consumer might feel the waiting experience wasn't as bad as originally thought. In such a case, the consumer's tolerance will be higher next time because she understands the restaurant is worth the wait.

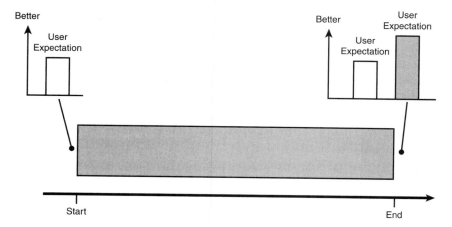

FIGURE 10.13

Making sure that users' perception of the quality of your solution surpasses their expectation builds tolerance.

KEEPING IN MIND

There is a mental threshold beyond which a majority of people are not willing to wait. People unfamiliar with or unconvinced of the value of waiting will likely be those who won't even want to wait. For those who decide to start to wait, uncertainty (lack of information about the wait, for example) quickly eats up any patience and tolerance. Some businesses are known to artificially add a delay to their service to create a hunger (sometimes literally) for the service. (Think "Soup Nazi" episode of *Seinfeld*!) Remember that this is a delicate feat that should be tried only when your product or service has reached some critical acclaim!

Buffer and Offer

Offer to users what they can begin to use or consume before the entire solution or product is fully available. The best example of this is streaming videos over the Internet—you do not have to wait for the download of the entire video file to start watching it.

HOW AND WHY IT WORKS

This works simply because users have to wait less. Many applications, for instance, do not need to be loaded entirely before users can interact with them. Consider, for instance, a large application that has multiple function components, such as an e-mail program. When users start an e-mail program, they most likely want to do just a few things immediately despite the array of features that the program offers. If the e-mail program is fairly sophisticated and takes time to load, it makes sense to load what users might expect to use immediately (check new e-mail, compose new message, etc.) followed by the other features that might not be needed immediately (option settings, configure new accounts, spell-check, etc.).

KEEPING IN MIND

Some features that users want to use might take on a dependency or two on another part of the program, so a good exercise is to map out what is technically feasible against users' priorities and usage patterns. For solutions like streaming content, some math is necessary to determine how much to buffer so users do not "catch up" to the ongoing current progress (see Figure 10.14).

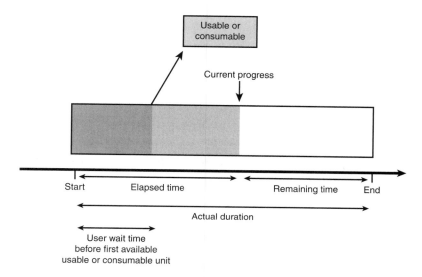

FIGURE 10.14

In the example above, when one usable or consumable part of the solution is ready, it becomes available to the user. This technique is commonly used in Web video and audio streaming solutions, but is also applicable to non-web solutions, such as client-based applications.

First-Time, One-Time Only

Some solutions will have delays that exist only when the solution is started up for the first time. In these instances, inform the user that this is a one-time delay that happens only when the solution is loaded or started for the very first time.

HOW AND WHY IT WORKS

This technique is effective because it gives users the information (more specifically, a reasonable explanation of delay) to build tolerance. This is not different from explaining you were late because you were unfamiliar with a new location. This technique should be used only one time. Beyond that, it will begin to sound more like a lame excuse!

KEEPING IN MIND

The situation described above and shown in Figure 10.15 should be distinguished from cold-start situations. A *cold start* refers to an instance when an application has to be launched (say, when the computer boots in the morning). Subsequent launches (perhaps during the day) are referred to as warm starts. Some applications are susceptible to slow cold starts because specific components of the applications need to be loaded into memory. Once in memory, subsequent launches are faster. There might be remedies to slow cold starts, such as preloading the required components, which is essentially a prelaunch warm-up. This ought to be considered carefully, however, especially if the warm-up takes a toll on the performance of applications.

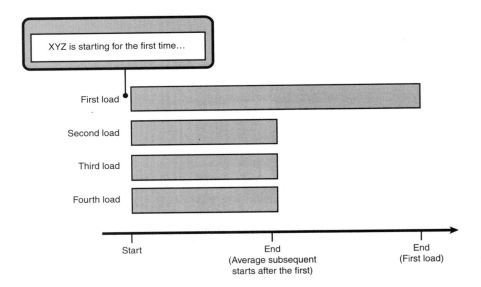

FIGURE 10.15

The example above shows an example when the first load of a solution is inevitably slow but subsequent loads are relatively faster. In such instances, simply inform users that this is a one-time delay that occurs only when the solution is loaded or started for the very first time.

Contextualized Benchmarks

Provide benchmark information to users to help them understand the dependencies of your solution.

HOW AND WHY IT WORKS

Whereas many tolerance techniques persuade users to be tolerant, this technique essentially turns the table and gives the user an "it's not me, it's you" message. Figure 10.16 shows two examples. More accurately, it shifts the burden of performance from the solution itself to other dependencies, such as network bandwidth, system processor speed, memory, and so forth. One example is found in MathWork's Matlab. The technical computation software has an inbuilt function (called bench) that reports a slew of basic to advanced performance diagnostics relative to the user's machine. In doing so, Matlab controls the benchmarks to which it is evaluated against and emphasizes to the user that the application's performance is largely determined by the user's hardware. Likewise, many websites give users a range of estimated download times, which depend on the user's Internet connection. Other solutions choose to display system metrics that explicitly state the user computer's performance.

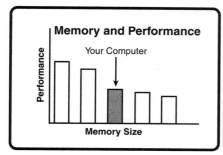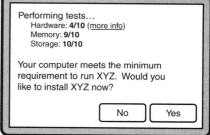

FIGURE 10.16

On the left, the solution informs the user how his or her computer matches up to computers of other configuration. Similarly, on the right, the solution explicitly gives the user a scorecard and informs the user if his or her system meets the minimum requirement of the installation of the solution.

KEEPING IN MIND

It is possible to include a "depending on your hardware" statement with an estimated range of duration. Remember that this technique shifts the burden to the user, so it should be done with some finesse. That is, make sure that nothing in the UI inadvertently communicates to users that their system is inferior. If a user's system is not optimal for your solution, always provide specifics about which aspect of the system is not optimal, such as the amount of memory or hard disk space and so forth.

End on Time

Give approximate remaining time in time anchors while a process is running, but when the process is actually complete, add a few seconds and show the process counting down to and ending exactly at zero (Figure 10.17).

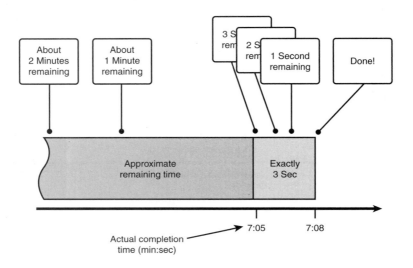

FIGURE 10.17

When a process is actually complete, add a few seconds and show the process counting down to and ending exactly at zero.

HOW AND WHY IT WORKS

This technique works because it creates an illusion of precision. Although it is not possible and advisable to show a countdown timer throughout the entire duration of a process, it is advantageous to show this at the end when you are certain that the process is completing. In this technique, the process has actually completed, but you are adding in a few seconds to show that the process is able to end precisely on zero.

KEEPING IN MIND

This works for relatively longer durations that run for at least several minutes. Adding five seconds to a ten-minute process is fairly negligible. Adding five seconds to a three-second process would be gratuitous.

Summary

This chapter introduces nine perceptual management techniques that must be considered to make the perception of actual durations shorter than it really is. When perception is too rigid to alter, tolerance management should be considered. The second half of the chapter introduces eight additional techniques that work by increasing user tolerance.

Rabbit Hole

Website-Related Studies

Bouch, A., A. Kuchinsky, and N. Bhatti (2000). Quality is in the eye of the beholder: Meeting users' requirements for Internet quality of service. In proceedings of the SIGCHI conference on human factors in computing systems, 297–304.

Dellaert, B. G. C. and B. E. Kahn (1999). How tolerable is delay consumers' evaluations of Internet websites after waiting. *Journal of Interactive Marketing,* 13, 41–54.

Rose, G. M., M. L. Meuter, and J. M. Curran (2005). On-line waiting: The role of download time and other important predictors on attitude toward e-retailers. *Psychology and Marketing,* 22, 127–151.

Ryan, G. and M. Valverde (2006). Waiting in line for online services: A qualitative study of the user's perspective. *Information Systems Journal,* 16, 181–211.

Waiting and Customer Satisfaction

Antonide, G., P. C. Verhoef, and M. van Aalst (2002). Consumer perception and evaluation of waiting time: A field experiment. *Journal of Consumer Psychology,* 12, 193–202.

David, M. M. and J. Heineke (1998). How disconfirmation, perception and actual waiting times impact customer satisfaction. *International Journal of Service Industry Management,* 9, 64–73.

Houston, M. B., Bettencourt. L. A. and S. Wenger (1998). The relationship between waiting in a service queue. *Psychology & Marketing,* 15, 735–753.

Maister, D.H. (1985). The psychology of waiting lines. In Czepiel (Ed.), *The Service Encounter.* Lexington, MA: Lexington Books, 113–123.

Pruyn, A. and A. Smidts (1999). Customers' reactions to waiting: Effects of the presence of 'fellow sufferers' in the waiting room. *Advances in Consumer Research,* 26, 211–216.

Unzicker, D. K. (1999). The psychology of being put on hold: An exploratory study of service quality. *Psychology & Marketing,* 16, 327–350.

Research and Techniques in the Consumer and Retail Worlds

Evangelist, S., B. Godwin, J. Johnson, V. Conzola, R. Kizer, S. Young-Helou, and R. Metters (2002). Linking marketing and operation: An application at Blockbuster, Inc. *Journal of Service Research,* 5, 91–100.

Hui, M. K. and D. K. Tse (1996). What to tell consumers in waits of different lengths: An integrative model of service evaluation. *Journal of Marketing,* 60, 81–90.

Katz, K. L., B. M. Larson, and R. C. Larson (1991). Prescriptions for the waiting in line blues: Entertain, enlighten and engage. *Sloan Management Review,* Winter, 44–53.

Kellaris, J. J. and R. J. Kent (1992). The influence of music on consumers' temporal perceptions: Does time fly when you're having fun? *Journal of Consumer Psychology,* 1, 365–376. Leclerc, F. (2002). How should one be told to hold. *Advances in Consumer Research,* 28, 78.

Leclerc, F. (2002). How should one be told to hold. *Advances in Consumer Research,* 28, 78.

North, A. C., D. J. Hargreaves, and J. McKendrick (1999). Music and on-hold waiting time. *British Journal of Psychology,* 90, 161–164.

Tansik, D. A. and R. Routhieaux (1999). Customer stress-relaxation: The impact of music in a hospital waiting room. *International Journal of Service Industry Management,* 10, 68–81.

Tom, G. and S. Lucey (1995). Waiting time delays and customer satisfaction in supermarkets. *Journal of Services Marketing,* 9, 20–29.

Violations

If it is possible to make time fly, it is also possible to make time crawl. Anything that causes actual durations to be perceived as longer than they really are or reduces user tolerance is a violation because it works against the optimal user experience. This chapter describes some of these violations and discusses some ways to prevent and correct them.

Perceptual Violations

Users do not typically carry a stopwatch to time every single interaction they make with the computer. Unless they are conducting tests, users are more likely to predict how long a particular interaction may take, approximately how long it has been running, or estimate how long some process took. The first types of violation are those that make users perceive that the actual duration taken by a process is longer than it really is. Many factors influence the perception of duration, and the following violations capture some of the factors that negatively affect the user experience:

- Watching the kettle
- Captive waits
- Negative appraisal
- Elapsed time

- Barnabus Effect
- Information overload
- Fragmented durations
- Anxiety

Watching the Kettle

Paying attention to a long-running process might cause the actual duration of the process to be overestimated (Figure 11.1).

HOW AND WHY IT VIOLATES

Why does the water in the kettle take more time to boil when it is being watched? Unless we are talking about drastic altitude differences, the same amount of water obviously boils at about the same time under the same conditions. What the idiom points out is that we are generally not used to witnessing the entirety of long-running processes and activities (water boiling in a kettle, clothes washing in a washer, pie baking in the oven, etc.) because we are more interested in when things complete.

Likewise, users are not used to watching the moment to moment of long-running progress and are more likely to periodically check whether the process has completed. Unless there is some action the user can take based on progress, such as stopping a search when a specific file has been found, the average user is likely more interested in the time of completion. When users watch the moment-to-moment progress without any indication of when it will complete, the tendency is to expect the next second to be the final one. This pain is the same as one that brews, no pun intended, when watching a kettle boil.

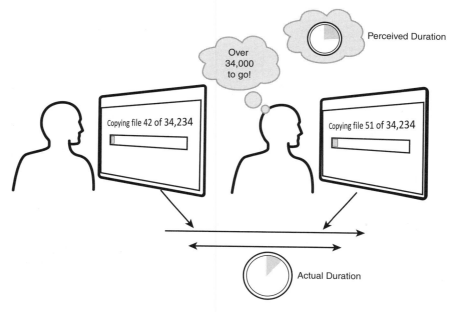

FIGURE 11.1

In this example, the user is watching the moment-to-moment progress of a copy operation. Watching the progress is, as the saying goes, watching the kettle boil.

KEEPING IN MIND

If there is no meaning, purpose, or value for the user to know the minutia of the process, don't show it. Chapter 6, "Progress Indication," gives some guidance on this. In addition, remember that we are accustomed to relying on cues or signals—the whistling of the kettle or the beep from the microwave—to tell us that something is complete or ready. This frees us to attend to other matters and tasks. Similarly, you should allow or encourage users to attend to other tasks while a long-running process in progress and offer to notify the user when the process is complete. An additional consideration is to give the option to perform a follow-up task (such as restarting the computer, closing the application, etc.) when the process completes.

Captive Waits

Any running process that holds the user's computer, operating system, or application "hostage" likely causes the captive time to be perceived longer than it really is.

HOW AND WHY IT VIOLATES

For safety reasons, some modern self-cleaning ovens lock themselves up during automatic cleaning. When the self-cleaning starts, the oven is held "captive" and cannot be used until the process finishes. Suppose you suddenly remember that you urgently need to use the oven after the self-cleaning has started. Every single second that passes without the self-cleaning completing is antagonizing, especially if there is no indication of when it will complete. In most cases, a task like the self-cleaning is voluntarily started by the user. This is much less painful than instances when a process starts unexpectedly, such as the Federal Communications Commission (FCC) mandatory "This is a test of the Emergency Alert System" that pops up while you are watching TV.

When users start an application, they typically have in mind a sequence of steps to accomplish some goal. Unexpected and especially untimely interruptions, such as the maintenance task shown in the preceding diagram, commandeer the application and essentially bring the user flow to a halt. In the user's mind, every passing second without being able to get back to the flow is a second wasted. Perceived wasted time passes more slowly than active time.

KEEPING IN MIND

Remember that it is not the actual time held captive by the process that causes users to overestimate how much time has elapsed. A solution may lock itself up to perform a task (like the one shown in Figure 11.2) for ten seconds, which may be excruciating to the user. However, the user might later spend more than 30 seconds deciding what adjective to use in an e-mail message. The former may be perceived as a waste, but the latter is not. It is really the subjective value of the time that determines whether the user feels that time has been wasted. Think back to the FCC's Emergency Alert System test. People would be less annoyed if the test were to always occur during commercials because the value of time during the show is more precious to the viewer than the value of time during commercials.

As a rule of thumb, any process that takes more than ten seconds should include a way for users to either stop the process or allow them to attend to other tasks (see Chapter 4, "Responsiveness"). For processes that take several minutes, consider minimizing the user interface (UI), encourage users to attend to other tasks, and present a notification when the process is complete.

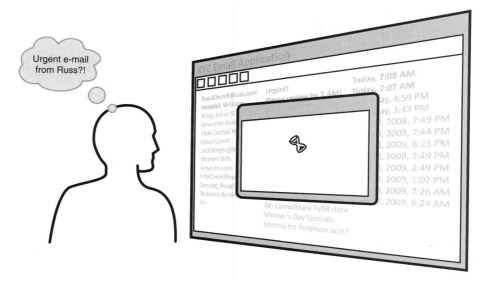

FIGURE 11.2

In this example, the XYZ e-mail application is preventing the user from interacting with the application while it is performing a maintenance task.

Negative Appraisal

Any intended or unintended indication on the UI that explicitly suggests that a process takes a long time causes users to form a perception of the process as being too time-consuming.

HOW AND WHY IT VIOLATES

Often, we determine how long something will take by looking at both direct and indirect indications in the environment. For example, suppose you are getting onto the highway and are greeted with bumper-to-bumper traffic. It would be reasonable to assume, based on the number of vehicles and the slow speed, that your drive will take longer than expected.

In the same way, users rely on direct indication, like progress indicators, and indirect indications on the UI to get an idea about how much time something takes. Users want to get some estimate of the time because it allows them to prioritize, plan ahead, and attend to other tasks (checking for new messages, taking a bathroom break, etc.). The visible information on the UI is the first and most direct indication for the user. If users perceive, incorrectly or not, that the process will take too much time (such as the two examples shown in Figure 11.3), there is a risk they might not even want to start the process.

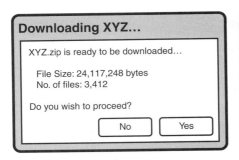
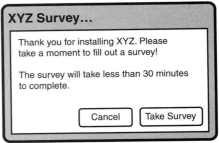

FIGURE 11.3

The UI on the left is using some huge numbers for units the user might not understand, and the UI on the right is projecting a long duration that seems unreasonable for a survey. Both examples cause the user to assume the worst and hesitate or resist proceeding.

KEEPING IN MIND

Always consider the level of information the user needs to see. Mainstream users might only need to know how long the process takes, but savvier users might want to know how much disk space or other resources it consumes. If you have a mix of users, consider progressive disclosure. (See the "Progress Unit" section in Chapter 6.)

Elapsed Time

Any indication on the UI that tells users how much time has elapsed without any other purpose only serves as a sore reminder of how much time has gone by.

HOW AND WHY IT VIOLATES

Related to the "watching the kettle" violation, this violation reminds us that we typically don't need to and don't want to pay attention to the moment-to-moment progress in the many long-running activities in life unless there is a reason to use elapsed time to make a decision. Sometimes tracking elapsed time is useful and sometimes critical (such as when cooking, operating machines, making an expensive phone call, etc.) For many other activities and processes, particularly a service-related industry, reporting elapsed time can do more harm than good because it serves as a constant and sore reminder of how long people have waited (Figure 11.4).

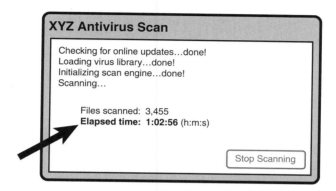

FIGURE 11.4

In this example, the UI for an antivirus scanning program is reporting how much time has elapsed. In most cases, this information only serves as a reminder to the user of how much time has gone by.

Similarly in human-computer interaction, unless it is meaningful for the user to take some action based on elapsed time, elapsed time is a reminder of time passed without completion. As mentioned in a previous violation, users are more likely to want to know when something finishes.

KEEPING IN MIND

Do not use elapsed time just because remaining time cannot be determined. The section on remaining time in Chapter 7, "Expressing Time," provides further guidance on this. The first choice should always be to give users an indication of when something will complete. In addition, consider reporting work units completed (phase completed, tables searched, etc.) or work remaining (phase to be completed, tables to be searched, etc.). Read Chapters 6 and 7 for more tips.

Barnabus Effect

The first experience of a new or unfamiliar process is prone to be perceived as longer than subsequent experiences.

HOW AND WHY IT VIOLATES

Barnabus is the name of a lab rat at Brown University who could perform a sequence of impressive tricks to get to a food reward. When a short video clip of Barnabus performing his feat was shown to people two times, well over 90% of the viewers indicated that the second video playback was shorter than the first. This has nothing to do with the uniqueness of the rat's skills and everything to do with how our brains process information and how that mental workload affects time perception. This is commonly experienced when we drive to a location for the second time; we swear that the first drive seemed longer (Figure 11.5).

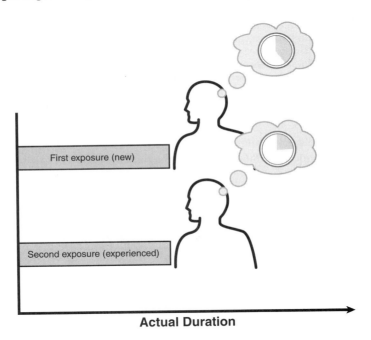

Actual Duration

FIGURE 11.5

Because the mind is more active in processing the experience of a new and unfamiliar process, its duration is frequently perceived longer than a second experience although both might be objectively equal.

Most interactions with the computer are meant to be performed several times (such as downloading, search, antivirus scanning, etc.), whereas a handful of others are meant to be performed ideally once or only a few times (such as installation, system configuration, etc.). The Barnabus Effect comes into play in the former when users have to repeat an interaction when the first experience is judged to be longer than subsequent experiences. It is probable that our brains at harder at work when we experience something novel; when we are familiar with what are experiencing, fewer mental processes are involved. This difference in how we mentally process the two experiences likely affects our time perception of both experiences.

KEEPING IN MIND

Remember that this is an effect that is possible only when users pay attention to the details in the first experience and when there are two or more experiences to compare. Therefore, a possible way to prevent the Barnabus Effect is to make that comparison not possible by turning the user's attention away from the process itself. The Barnabus Effect should be distinguished from instances when the first launch of an application is indeed measurably slow. Some applications do start slower upon the initial launch but load up significantly faster upon subsequent launches. In such instances when there is a "cold-start" slack, it is wise to warn users the slack is to be expected and assure them subsequent launches will be faster.

Information Overload

Overloading users with too much information about a process during the process itself can cause perception of duration to be inaccurate.

HOW AND WHY IT VIOLATES

Overloading users with too much information can cause the duration of the process to be perceived longer than it really is. First, when people pay attention to nontime-related information of an event, perception of time-related information (duration, for example) is distorted. Conversely, when people pay attention to time-related information of an event, perception of time-related information (details of process, for example) is compromised. This tradeoff is described in a theory called the *Attenuation Hypothesis*.

When the UI shows a constant stream of information, such as the one shown in Figure 11.6, the user's attention is naturally drawn toward it. To the average user, this fluttering activity on the UI steals attention from and distorts the perception of time. The end result is typically an overestimation of the actual duration.

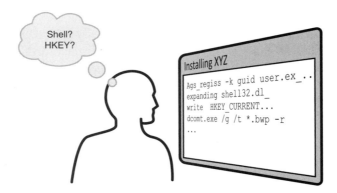

FIGURE 11.6

In the example above, the UI of an installation program is reporting details that are mean-ingless or overwhelming to the user. When users have to pay attention to these minute details, perception of time is commonly compromised.

KEEPING IN MIND

Remember that this is not exactly about the amount of information per se, but rather what the information means to the user. The same information can be an overload to someone who does not understand it, but not so to another person who understands it. Therefore, filling a duration with information can make time be perceived longer (than the same duration that is "empty") or shorter depending on the nature and value of that information to the user. For each piece of information you want to show on the UI, ask what your typical user can realistically do with the information given.

Fragmented Durations

Interruptions break a single process into multiple parts, which are prone to be perceived longer than one that is remembered as a whole or made up of fewer parts (Figure 11.7).

HOW AND WHY IT VIOLATES

When a process or activity is divided into parts, instead of remembering one continuous event, people remember the multiple small parts that made up the whole. The danger in remembering separate parts is what Gestalt psychology teaches: The whole is larger than the sum of the parts. To look at this from a more meaningful perspective, Gestalt psychology is saying that our brains use parts to form an overall perception of some-thing that is larger than it really is. Take a typical 30-minute TV show as an example.

Although we know the commercials probably account for a third of the show from start to finish, we perceive that it is a half-hour show and don't talk, for instance, about how we enjoyed the full 20 minutes of our favorite TV show last night.

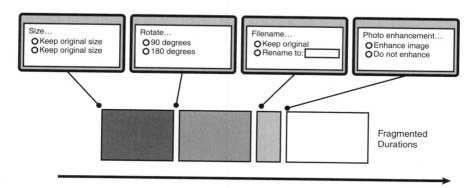

FIGURE 11.7

In this example, a single process is broken into separate parts by the intermittent requests for user input.

In human-computer interaction, when a single process consists of multiple checkpoints that require a user's attention and feedback, the single process is essentially broken into multiple processes (in the user's mind) each with its own duration. The more steps and checkpoints that users remember, the more chunks of durations that are pooled together to estimate how long the process lasted.

KEEPING IN MIND

This violation relates to long-running tasks that can really be carried out without intermittent breaks that request user input. Examples include installations and long-running scans or searches. This violation also applies to some relatively longer-running wizard UIs that guide users through a process. Ideally, wizards should guide a user through a series of decisions, and then perform the necessary operations as a whole after all the user information has been collected.

An added advantage in making such process more seamless is to prevent the unpleasant experience of starting a long-running process with the confidence it will be done when you come back from your break. Alas, upon your return, you find a "Are you really sure you want to proceed?" dialog waiting for your response.

Anxiety

Under stressful or highly emotive states, perception of time is heavily distorted, and delays are typically magnified.

HOW AND WHY IT VIOLATES

Some U.S. soldiers in the Middle East carry handheld voice-translation devices that help them overcome language barriers and communicate with the locals. Many applications and solutions are meant to be mission critical or used in situations where there is high stress. Research has shown that under stressful or highly emotive states, people tend to have poor judgment of time. For example, if there is some urgency (such as the example in Figure 11.8) to consume or receive some information, every single second is extremely precious, and therefore every second of delay seems to pass extremely slowly.

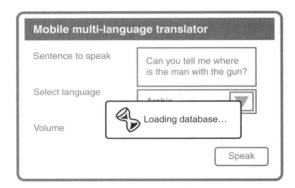

FIGURE 11.8

Imagine if a soldier is in a very urgent situation where he needs to get a sentence translated. Upon entering the sentence and clicking Speak, the application locks up to load a language database.

KEEPING IN MIND

For applications that may be used in a situation when the user is in a mission-critical context or in an environment with some level of stress, it is always advisable to aim for simplicity over complexity. Another perfect example is the application that runs police squad cars. Police officers must interact with the application to retrieve critical information in possibly high-stress environments, and interruptions to accomplishing the task must be minimized.

Tolerance Violations

Some violations do not cause actual time to be perceived longer than it really is. Rather, they cause users to lose patience and tolerance. As mentioned in Chapter 2, "Perception and Tolerance," tolerance can be affected by both factors inherent in the UI (such as using the wrong progress indication and so on) or by factors typically beyond your control (such as the reputation of the brand name and so forth). This section focuses on what is within your control to identify and correct:

- Uncertainty
- Broken promises
- Cable company commitment
- Overprecision
- Loop confirmation
- Surprise supplement
- Delayed consumption

Uncertainty

Not giving users any indication or information about when a process will complete causes time to be perceived as passing more slowly.

HOW AND WHY IT VIOLATES

As far as violations are concerned, many lines of research have identified uncertainty as the biggest culprit. Apart from the fact that we are by and large impatient, not knowing how long some process takes makes it difficult for us to multitask, prioritize, and plan ahead. In the two examples shown in Figure 11.9, there is no indication of how long the application will take if started, and worst, once started, when it ends. Forcing users to start a process without telling them how long it will take is as bad as forcing someone to commit to buy something without telling them how much it costs.

KEEPING IN MIND

The best cure to uncertainty is certainty. Always aim to provide some information to give users some level of certainty whenever possible. As mentioned in Chapter 6, both time units and work units can be considered.

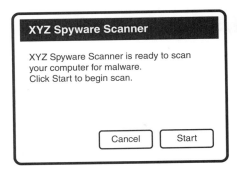 

FIGURE 11.9

In the example on the left, there is no indication of how long the spyware scan will take. In the example on the right, there is no indication of how much progress has been made or how much more time is needed.

Broken Promises

When a process goes beyond the duration as estimated or promised by the UI, user tolerance is negatively affected.

HOW AND WHY IT VIOLATES

Naturally, when a process takes longer than what was promised, user tolerance will be reduced. Remember that users use the information you provide in the UI to prioritize, plan ahead, and multitask. Suppose a user has exactly five minutes before he must leave the office to catch a bus, and an installation, such as the one shown in Figure 11.10, is promising that the installation will take only five minutes. Five minutes goes by, and the installation has not completed. Although the user was able to tolerate the first five minutes, his tolerance for any additional time taken beyond that is extremely reduced.

KEEPING IN MIND

Think of tolerance as a mental budget users set aside before they engage or start a process. When your application eats up that budget, you are walking on thin ice. Therefore, be careful with what you promise on the UI because users assume that the time estimate is accurate and use that information to prioritize and multitask.

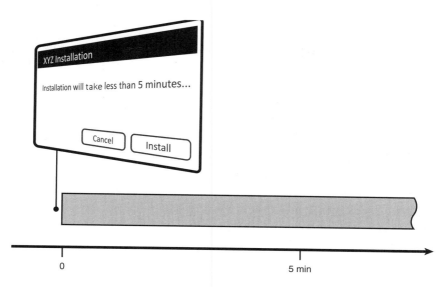

FIGURE 11.10

In this example, the UI indicates that it will take less than five minutes. However, the process has gone past the time indicated. Tolerance beyond the time promised is understandably reduced.

Cable Company Commitment

When the estimated range of duration is too wide, tolerance is reduced even before the process begins (Figure 11.11).

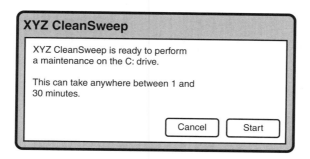

FIGURE 11.11

In this example, a maintenance application is estimating a range that is too wide to be useful for the user.

HOW AND WHY IT VIOLATES

Cable companies have gotten a bad rap about this violation, but other service providers are also notorious in giving unreasonably wide estimated duration. This violation doesn't relate to uncertainty because there is some level of certainty that the promised service will happen in a specific time frame. The problem is the length of the time frame itself. The wider the window of estimated time, the more people feel the estimates given reflect the noncommittal nature or even laziness of the service provider.

KEEPING IN MIND

Keep in mind that cable companies can get away with stating wide ranges because consumers don't really have any other choice. Consider a different situation when you need a plumber. Chances are you will hang up the phone laughing if the plumber states that he can be there between 9 a.m. and 4 p.m. When users have no choice, tolerance is a little higher (but it doesn't mean they are not annoyed!). When they do have choices, tolerance is extremely slim if existent at all.

Overprecision

An overly precise projected time of completion invites users to put the precision to the test.

HOW AND WHY IT VIOLATES

Some customer service call centers give users an automated estimation of how much time callers have to wait before they can reach a live operator. What would be a likely response if the automated voice announces that you will reach a live operator in 3 minutes and 35 seconds? It would not be surprising if you feel like grabbing a stopwatch to actually time the wait. People tend to gravitate to particular numbers when estimating and expressing time. (See the discussion about time anchors in Chapter 7.) In the example shown in Figure 11.12, the UI is indicating that the maintenance will take exactly 8.5 minutes. Using precise units gives the impression that the given time estimates are exact, which invites users to put that precision to the test.

KEEPING IN MIND

Unless there is a need for the user to see precise units, there is no reason to use precise time units. Even if it is true and reliable that the process takes a specific time to complete, such as the example shown in Figure 11.12, round up to the next higher time anchor and indicate that the process takes less than that time anchor, such as "less than ten minutes."

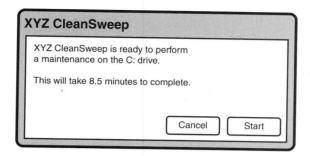

FIGURE 11.12

In this example, a maintenance application is promising the process will take exactly 8.5 minutes to complete. Reporting exact completion times invites users to put the precision to the test.

Loop Confirmation

A common practice to fill up time during long-running processes, especially installations, is to display a finite series of preset information in the UI. However, when the series finishes and restarts at the beginning, the cycling of the series reduces user tolerance (Figure 11.13).

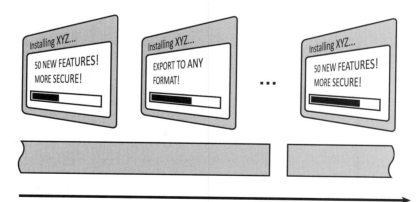

FIGURE 11.13

In this example, during the installation of an application, a series of slides about the new features of the software displays. However, when the series runs out, the installation process returns to the first slide.

HOW AND WHY IT VIOLATES

Everyone is familiar with the experience of being placed on hold on the phone and hearing a recording like "Your call is important to us." This initially conveys a sense of assurance, but it becomes annoying when we begin to hear the same message repeated over and over again. This is similar to the experience in theaters when they start to repeat the brainteasers and advertisement slides before the movie begins. People begin to use noticeable repetitions as time markers to gauge the passage of time.

Many long-running tasks, as shown in Figure 11.13, incorporate a series of slide shows that repeats for as long as the task is running. Although this is initially effective in diverting users' attention from the duration of the actual process, repeats actually begin to reduce tolerance like "Your call is important to us" does.

KEEPING IN MIND

Although solutions like the slide show shown in Figure 11.13 are designed to make time pass faster, they can have a reverse effect if the information is of no value to the user. Diversion, as mentioned in Chapter 10, "Techniques," works when some user interaction is possible or when information presented is meaningful and valuable to the user.

Surprise Supplement

When users are not warned about a process that follows another, their tolerance for the unexpected process is greatly reduced (Figure 11.14).

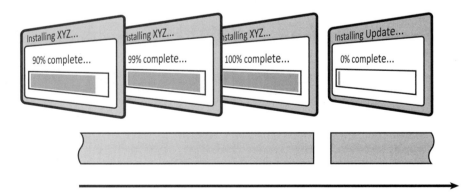

FIGURE 11.14

In this example, the user is expecting the installation to complete once it hits 100%. Unfortunately, there was an additional update installation the user wasn't aware of. Tolerance for this unexpected process is low.

HOW AND WHY IT VIOLATES

Famous comedian Jerry Seinfeld had a funny joke about the waiting room in the doctor's office: "They finally call you…so you think you're going to see the doctor, but you're not, are you? No. You're going into the next waiting room—the littler waiting room." People like to mentally prepare for a long wait before it begins. When they are surprised by additional wait time, it is almost as if their tolerance is depleted.

In human-computer interactions, a great example of this violation is found in many application installations that require multiple installations of supporting technologies. When users are not aware that a series of installations are required, they may assume the first is the only installation required. When an unexpected second process starts, user tolerance for that "surprise supplement" is greatly reduced.

KEEPING IN MIND

An old salesman trick calls for you to get your foot in the door and ask for a little from potential buyers before reeling them in for more. Some college professors are notorious for doing the same—promising that the quiz has only five questions, but not mentioning that each question comprises ten parts! This should never be a principle for software design—where you deliberately choose not to reveal additional processes that are involved in hopes of "reeling them into" your solution. Be explicit about what is required for the application or solution to be operational or consumable.

Delayed Consumption

When users feel they are forbidden to start using a solution because it has not loaded all its features, many of which the users do not need immediately, tolerance is reduced.

HOW AND WHY IT VIOLATES

Suppose you get to a store or a shop (perhaps Starbucks) minutes before they open for business. You can clearly see the staff getting things ready. If you happen to have a serious craving for a coffee, every second that goes by watching the staff taking their sweet time and you not getting your caffeine fix is excruciating.

There is a parallel example in the software world. Most applications launch systematically in a preset sequence, and once all components are ready, the application is then ready for the user (Figure 11.15). The more complex the application, the longer the sequence will be. The longer the launch time, the longer users have to wait to start using the application. When users can see a component that has already been loaded but can't use it, or when other components are loaded and ready but they are irrelevant to the user, tolerance is negatively affected.

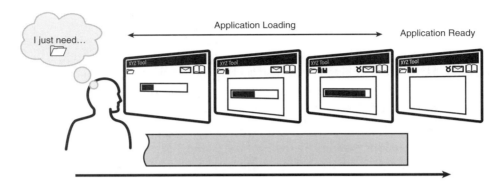

FIGURE 11.15

The application shown in this diagram is loading the components to get to a fully ready state. This is annoying for the user who really wants to perform a simple task but has to wait for the entire application to be fully loaded before he can use the application.

KEEPING IN MIND

Create a list of functions or tasks that users can do with the application and prioritize them according to the probability of their use (that is, how likely each function or task would be needed by the user when the application starts). For example, for an e-mail program, checking for new mail, composing new e-mail, finding existing e-mail, and such should rank high on the list. Aim to load up the components necessary to accomplish these high-probability functions or tasks and allow users to interact with the application while the low-probability parts are prepared.

Summary

This chapter introduces 15 common violations that can be prevented or corrected. The first eight are perceptual violations because they cause actual durations to be perceived longer than it really is. The remaining seven are termed tolerance violations because they all cause users to be less patient, less forgiving, and less tolerant of a wait or a delay.

Rabbit Hole

Underestimations and Overestimations

Goodin, R. E., J. M. Rice, M. Bittman, M., and P. Saunders (2005). The time-pressure illusion: Discretionary time vs. free time. *Social Indicators Research,* 73, 43–70.

Hancock, P. A. and J. L. Weaver (2005). On time distortion under stress. *Theoretical Issues in Ergonomics Science,* 6, 193–211.

Loftus, E. F. (1987). Time went by so slowly: Overestimation of event duration by males and females. *Applied Cognitive Psychology,* 1, 3–13.

Mattes, S. and R. Ulrich (1998). Directed attention prolongs the perceived duration of a brief stimulus. *Perception & Psychophysics,* 60, 1305–1317.

Roy, M. M., N. J. S. Christenfeld, and C. R. M. McKenzie (2005). Underestimating the duration of future events memory incorrectly used or memory bias. *Psychological Bulletin,* 131, 738–756.

Yarmey, A. D. (2000). Retrospective duration estimations for variant and invariant events in field situations. *Applied Cognitive Psychology,* 14, 45–57.

Waiting and Customer Satisfaction

Antonide, G., P. C. Verhoef, and M. van Aalst (2002). Consumer perception and evaluation of waiting time: A field experiment. *Journal of Consumer Psychology,* 12, 193–202.

David, M. M. and J. Heineke (1998). How disconfirmation, perception and actual waiting times impact customer satisfaction. *International Journal of Service Industry Management,* 9, 64–73.

Houston, M. B., L. A. Bettencourt, and S. Wenger (1998). The relationship between waiting in a service queue. *Psychology & Marketing,* 15, 735–753.

Pruyn, A. and A. Smidts (1999). Customers' reactions to waiting: Effects of the presence of 'fellow sufferers' in the waiting room. *Advances in Consumer Research,* 26, 211–216.

Unzicker, D. K. (1999). The psychology of being put on hold: An exploratory study of service quality. *Psychology & Marketing,* 16, 327–350.

Index

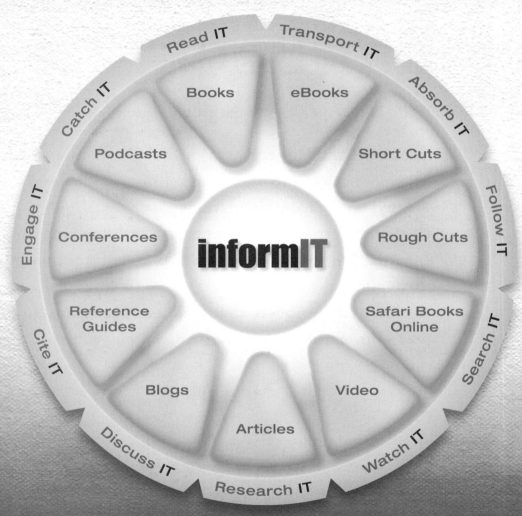

LearnIT at InformIT

Go Beyond the Book

Read IT — Books

Transport IT — eBooks

Absorb IT — Short Cuts

Catch IT — Podcasts

Engage IT — Conferences

Follow IT — Rough Cuts

Cite IT — Reference Guides

Search IT — Safari Books Online

Discuss IT — Blogs

Watch IT — Video

Research IT — Articles

informIT

11 WAYS TO LEARN IT at **www.informIT.com/learn**

The online portal of the information technology
publishing imprints of Pearson Education

 Addison Wesley · **Cisco Press** · EXAM✓**CRAM** · **IBM Press** · **que** · PRENTICE HALL **SAMS**

Safari Library
Subscribe Now!
http://safari.informit.com/library

Safari's entire technology collection is now available with no restrictions. Imagine the value of being able to search and access thousands of books, videos, and articles from leading technology authors whenever you wish.

EXPLORE TOPICS MORE FULLY

Gain a more robust understanding of related issues by using Safari as your research tool. With Safari Library you can leverage the knowledge of the world's technology gurus. For one flat, monthly fee, you'll have unrestricted access to a reference collection offered nowhere else in the world—all at your fingertips.

With a Safari Library subscription, you'll get the following premium services:

- **Immediate access to the newest, cutting-edge books**—Approximately eighty new titles are added per month in conjunction with, or in advance of, their print publication.

- **Chapter downloads**—Download five chapters per month so you can work offline when you need to.

- **Rough Cuts**—A service that provides online access to prepublication information on advanced technologies. Content is updated as the author writes the book. You can also download Rough Cuts for offline reference

- **Videos**—Premier design and development videos from training and e-learning expert lynda.com and other publishers you trust.

- **Cut and paste code**—Cut and paste code directly from Safari. Save time. Eliminate errors.

- **Save up to 35% on print books**—Safari Subscribers receive a discount of up to 35% on publishers' print books.

Addison Wesley · Cisco Press · Microsoft Press · Peachpit Press · Redbooks

Adobe Press · FT Press FINANCIAL TIMES · New Riders · PRENTICE HALL · Wharton School Publishing · SAMS

  ALPHA · lynda.com · O'REILLY · que · IBM Press

Safari Books Online

Safari®

BOOKS ONLINE

ENABLED

THIS BOOK IS SAFARI ENABLED

INCLUDES FREE 45-DAY ACCESS TO THE ONLINE EDITION

The Safari® Enabled icon on the cover of your favorite technology book means the book is available through Safari Bookshelf. When you buy this book, you get free access to the online edition for 45 days.

Safari Bookshelf is an electronic reference library that lets you easily search thousands of technical books, find code samples, download chapters, and access technical information whenever and wherever you need it.

TO GAIN 45-DAY SAFARI ENABLED ACCESS TO THIS BOOK:

- Go to **informit.com/safarienabled**

- Complete the brief registration form

- Enter the coupon code found in the front of this book on the "Copyright" page

WITHDRAWN

If you have difficulty registering on Safari Bookshelf or accessing the online edition, please e-mail customer-service@safaribooksonline.com.